Is a PhD for Me?

Life in the Ivory Tower: A Cautionary Guide for Aspiring Doctoral Students

Yuval Bar-Or, PhD

TLB Publishing

Springfield, New Jersey

www.TLBcorp.com

Cover art: © iStockphoto.com/Ryan Burke

Jacket arranged by: Ralph Samson

Library of Congress Control Number: 2009900395

Library of Congress Cataloging-in-Publication Data

Bar-Or, Yuval, 1967–

   Is a PhD for Me? Life in the Ivory Tower: A Cautionary Guide for Aspiring Doctoral Students / Yuval Bar-Or

   p.   cm.

Includes bibliographical references, tables and index.

   ISBN: 978-0-9800118-1-4

   1. PhD. 2. Doctor of Philosophy. 3. Graduate Education. 4. Academic Careers. 5. Ivory Tower. I. Title.

Printed in the United States of America

Dedicated to Marilyn Bar-Or

Acknowledgements

I thank John Schindler for detailed feedback on the penultimate version of the manuscript, as well as the National Opinion Research Center (NORC), the U.S. Department of Education's National Center for Education Statistics (NCES), and the American Association of University Professors (AAUP) for allowing me to present some of their data. I also thank Kate Steele for her editorial work, and Bareket Falk and Heather Cluley for feedback on early versions of the manuscript.

Table of Contents

Education is an admirable thing, but it is well to remember from time to time that nothing worth knowing can be taught.

- Oscar Wilde

Author's Note

Over the years, beginning when I was a PhD student, people have been approaching me to inquire about the PhD process. Invariably, they want to know what the academic life is really like, and whether the PhD is right for them. In a sense, this book is my comprehensive response to those questions.

As I was writing this book, a friend asked me, "Will the book be 'pro' or 'con' the academic world?" Until that moment, it hadn't occurred to me that the book might be interpreted as one or the other for a simple reason—I had no intention of making a negative or positive statement.

This book is intended as a constructive review, offering insight into the inner workings of academic institutions—an insular, occasionally misunderstood segment of society. I hope you will gain an appreciation of the academic world and its contributions to humanity, along with an understanding of its current weaknesses and deficiencies.

Affirmative action and the declining quality of education are among the topics discussed: these controversial subjects are included primarily to help paint the academic landscape and its major outstanding issues. I don't claim to provide comprehensive coverage of these and other topics. In nearly all cases I have attempted a neutral view, presenting the issues as objectively as possible.

Introduction

According to the *Columbia Encyclopedia*, the Doctor of Philosophy, or *Philosophiae Doctoris* in Latin, is a "title bestowed upon a student on the fulfillment of certain requirements or given as an honor to an eminent person. The practice of awarding degrees originated in the universities of medieval Europe. The first known degree, granted to doctoral candidates in civil law, was awarded in Italy at the University of Bologna during the 12th century."[1]

The National Opinion Research Center reported that 48,079 PhDs were awarded in 2007 across the United States of America. Yet, this large number significantly underestimates the annual total of people who have an interest in pursuing doctoral studies. First, it reflects only those who graduate, not those who originally enroll. Second, it doesn't include those who are initially interested in enrolling, but decide to abstain or are rejected.

Rough attrition assumptions indicate that 30-50 percent of an incoming class of graduate students fail to graduate. Using the 2007 graduating cohort and these crude attrition assumptions, one may estimate that originally between 68,000 and 96,000 students enrolled in PhD programs nationally; of those, between 20,000 to 48,000 students left school without the coveted degree. It's much harder to quantify those rejected and the abstainers, or the reasons the latter elected not to pursue graduate studies. Nevertheless, the point is that every year, thousands of talented people make an important career decision about pursuing the highest academic credential offered by our society, and many appear to make the wrong decision.

These observations raise an immediate question: what is the cost to society when such a large number of students fail to complete their academic goals, or abstain from such programs despite having the ability to thrive and contribute to the academic field?

The simple answer: the costs are extreme, including lost opportunity and lost productivity. The opportunity cost to society is significant sums of money and faculty resources spent on people who do not survive the process. Those resources could have been spent on others who would have succeeded and contributed to the academic community, and, in turn, to society. Lost productivity—when capable people remain outside the academic community, regardless of the reason—is likely proportional to the value society gains from those who do complete their advanced studies. Consider the advances in science and medicine during the last century: now, try to imagine how much *greater* our advancement would be if all those capable of contributing had succeeded in the academic community!

If a better mechanism existed to select students more likely to complete the program, reject those most likely to fail, and encourage abstainers to apply, society would benefit to the tune of billions of dollars because there would be far greater efficiency in the system of higher education. Grants, loans, and scholarships would be put to better use; professors' time would be most efficiently spent educating subsequent generations of academics. They, in turn, would contribute discoveries and effectively educate future generations of productive, moral citizens.

Accepting that the cost to society is high leads, in turn, to three other questions:

1. How can the abstainers be brought into the process so they, too, may contribute their natural talents by pursuing doctoral degrees and taking their place in institutions of higher learning and research?

2. What reasons or factors account for the failure of students to complete PhD programs?

3. Can such factors be dealt with earlier in the process, allowing more students to realize success?

The short answer to the first question is that many people fail to participate because they simply don't know enough about academia to know whether it is the correct career choice for them. The solution, therefore, is to do a better job informing them about such careers.

As for the second question, the often-assumed cause—that some incoming students just aren't smart enough—may only account for a small fraction of the total. Other reasons may include: personal distractions (including a death in the family, divorce, birth of a child, or the need to help with a family business), financial difficulties, lack of focus, lack of maturity, disdain for the academic life, lack of passion for the subject, insufficient technical preparation (lack of prerequisite courses), as well as the presence of other, more compelling opportunities seen as too important and impossible to pass up.

In response to the third question (and applicable to the others as well), the key to success is to overcome one challenge—the simple lack of understanding of the realities of academe. These are not issues of mental capacity, moral fiber, or good citizenship. They are mostly issues of insufficient information. The existing literature on graduate education focuses almost exclusively on gaining entry into a graduate program, but doesn't help prospective students decide whether they should pursue PhD studies or not. Thus, this book changes the focus from *how* to get into a graduate school, to an emphasis on *whether* one should go.

This book is meant to provide you, the aspiring academic, with detailed insight which can help with the decision to pursue graduate work, and, in the event that decision is made, to best equip you for the challenges ahead. The objective is to reveal the challenges in a doctoral program, the academic lifestyle, its inner workings, as well as identifying current issues confronting the academic community. These include the academic community's role in society, whether and how the ivory tower has failed the world, where education is headed, the role and effects of technological innovation, affirmative action, separation of church and state, freedom of expression, and ethics.

The content has been gleaned from dozens of interviews with current and former academics, spanning higher education experiences across faculties, countries, and genders. In making the decision to join the academic community, you must keep in mind that you may be a student for five or six years, but an academic for thirty years or more. Before committing to the rigors of a PhD program of study, you should know what it's like to be a researcher and professor, what it means to be a member of the broader academic community, and what your role will be within that community.

Who would find this book useful?

- Anyone considering graduate studies
- Anyone considering an academic career
- Advisors and principal investigators who mentor students and want to ensure their guidance is most effective
- Non-academics who are curious about the goings-on within the mysterious ivory tower

This book is exclusively about graduate studies leading to a doctoral (PhD) degree, not professional graduate degrees such as medicine (MD), law (JD), or business (MBA).

The book proceeds as follows: the first chapter plunges the reader into a week in the life of a young professor. The objective is to introduce aspiring students to what their life will be like after the doctoral program. Subsequent chapters describe the important phases of a doctoral program, including coursework, dissertation research, financial considerations, postdoctoral fellowships (as relevant) and the employment search. The next few chapters strive to paint the academic landscape, sketching out the role of the academic community in society, the administrative structure of an institution of higher learning, life in the ivory tower, and major current issues of importance to the academic community. Sufficiently enlightened, it is assumed the reader is now in a better position to decide whether the PhD is the appropriate path. Accordingly, the final chapters provide detailed checklists covering the application process and the decisions facing the student once acceptance is granted.

Chapter 1: A Week in the Life of a Young Professor

This section describes hypothetical, but quite representative, weekly activities of a young professor.

Monday

The professor strides into an early morning class and begins, unceremoniously, to scribble notes on a blackboard. He doesn't say good morning, doesn't take attendance, and doesn't apologize for being ten minutes late. An anxious student's request to receive photocopies of the professor's notes is refused. The professor grumbles, "If the notes were made available, no one would show up to class."

After an hour, the harried professor exits the classroom and makes his way to his office. One student follows the professor across the entire campus before getting up the courage to pull even with him and introduce himself as a member of the just-completed class, go on to explain he is interested in majoring in the subject and in being a research assistant. Torn between being annoyed and knowing that a number of shelved projects could be moved along with an assistant, the professor states, "I may have a need for one, but we'll have to wait a few weeks before I'll know if I have the budget. Why don't you email me in a few weeks?" The clinging student eventually lets up and heads off; the professor enters his office and settles in front of his computer. He quickly scans his email inbox and makes a mental note to renew his subscription to the field's leading journal (which he'll forget to do for another three weeks).

He continues to scan his email inbox, seeking news of his latest submission—this one to the most prestigious journal in the field. Once he convinces himself no response has arrived, he determines to ignore the other emails and instead focus on revisions to an older manuscript accepted by an editor at a slightly less-prestigious journal. He sent the manuscript seven months earlier and received the response only last week. Scanning the comments, he estimates it may take him three months to complete the requested revisions; he'll resubmit and hope that within another few months the revisions will be accepted. If all goes well, the publication would appear three to six months after that. It's a maddening process, but he is resigned to it.

These delays can be critical, as his tenure decision will be directly linked to the number of publications he amasses. The good news is the journal has accepted his paper; the bad news is the faculty committee may view this less-prestigious journal as insufficient to meet the requirements of tenure. *Oh, if the other submission is accepted by the leading journal, coupled with this article, I'll be in great shape.*

The professor sits down, beginning to focus on the revisions. It's been so long since he's thought about the paper, he has to concentrate deeply. Just as his thoughts begin to form, there is a feeble but noticeable knock on the door. A young face appears. The professor vaguely recognizes the student as one of the brighter attendees of last semester's class. With his mind still firmly on the revisions, he irritably acknowledges the pupil's presence. The latter senses the timing is bad, apologizes for the intrusion, suggests he will drop by again tomorrow, and withdraws.

Thank God for that, thinks the professor. Most intruders don't have the tact to withdraw so quickly.

The professor gets up and closes his door, realizing this will be another one of those days when he will pretend to be out, ignoring the people knocking on his door, because there is never enough time. He gets so caught up in thinking, he forgets he advertised the next hour as time set aside for students to see him. Several students make the effort, and depart—muttering about "irresponsible professors" who forget to honor their office hours. He will realize this only days later, when an irate student brings up the subject in class.

Finally, alone with his thoughts (thanks to a conditioned ability to ignore repeated knocks on his door), he manages to spend two reasonably productive hours responding to the referee's recommendations. A glance at the clock shows he's already a minute late for the next class. He stands up abruptly, sending his chair flying into a stack of photocopied journal articles behind him, and, without bothering to clean up the toppled mess, strides out. He backtracks once to grab a donut from a tray on the department secretary's desk. It represents lunch, although the thought that he's missing a decent lunch never even crosses his mind. Nutrition and health concerns haven't been on his radar for about eight years; his expanding waistline is proof.

The next two classes are taught back-to-back, and he can't even go to the bathroom between the two because several students besiege him. This semester, he is teaching three sections of the same course. Teaching three classes a day, two days a week, may be exhausting, but it could be worse. He taught three different courses simultaneously the previous year; the number of hours in class is the same, but each distinct course requires a lot of preparation time, teaching time and effort.

The first time around, endless hours were needed to create all the material for each course. Thereafter, it's not so bad from a time perspective, although each course requires a reasonable amount of time each year for updates. Roughly 20 percent of each course must be updated each year. Class prep is a demanding process: putting together class notes, creating sample test questions (with correct answers), outlining reading lists, and compiling questions to be used in examinations were so time-consuming he rarely had time to do anything other than prepare for class and teach. To make progress on his research, under constant pressure from the ticking tenure clock, he worked very long hours, often coming in to his office very early so he could get work done before students began to roam the halls.

Exhausted from the intensity of speaking for several hours straight, he fights his way past a cordon of students who want to ask questions about next week's midterm. He manages to escape after promising he will address their questions later in the week.

Returning to his office and spending another two hours on revisions, the professor is tired and hungry when he finally surfaces; a glance at the pantry yields the usual disappointment. The place is empty—no snacks. Knowing he must get some food, he heads to the basement cafeteria, praying no students will accost him with questions about exams or reading lists. Relieved, he returns from the sortie with a sandwich. He settles down for some tedious paperwork. A form he must fill in and submit to the department chair in order to process the purchase of a new computer to be used by his research assistant is on the top of the stack. The request is likely to meet with some level of disapproval from the bureaucrats; his research fund, several thousand dollars available annually to assist in his research efforts, does not have enough to cover the full costs of the new computer. He'll have to negotiate with the department chair, probably agreeing to a reduced fund for the following year. The next item is a short list of candidates for a visiting lecture series; the chairman thrust this duty upon him earlier in the year, arguing that this is a good way for him to complete his requirements of service to the university. He was assured this is important to his tenure decision, now only 15 months away. He scratches one of the names off the list, vetoed by one of the senior faculty members, who, the week before, pronounced said candidate a charlatan, unworthy of the title of academician. *Too bad*, thinks the professor, *I was really looking forward to hearing that talk.* But he knows he isn't sufficiently powerful to override the senior veto; the chairman doesn't have the energy to argue with the senior professor, either. "So much for the tolerance of the academic community," he laments.

The challenge now is to fill the vacated speaking slot. It's a tedious job, using various contacts to find people who could address important issues, and do so credibly, measuring up to the high standards of the senior faculty. He'd brought one person to the chairman's attention the previous week, but was told that, while the candidate is considered an expert in his field, his theories "wouldn't go over well in this department." *Whatever happened to academic openness to new ideas?* He makes a note to call some of his former classmates and ask whether there may be some good speaker candidates at their respective schools.

The next item is a memo reminding him he is on the selection committee for next year's incoming PhD student class. He is interested, but too tired to think much about it; he knows it will be hard work to filter through dozens of applications. On the other hand, he's looking forward to those few enthusiastic and serious applicants who remind him why he chose this career.

The final document is a reminder to register for an academic conference; he decides not to pay for registration at this stage, because there is still some chance an article he submitted months earlier will be accepted, which will mean a speaking slot at the conference. As a speaker, his registration fee will be waived. Without thinking it explicitly, he relishes the thought of being a speaker, and for a few moments indulges in the fantasy of himself, in his gray suit, a bright ribbon on his breast pocket identifying him as "Keynote Speaker."

Still clinging to the fantasy, he selects a handful of articles from one of the many stacks surrounding his desk, and, tucking the stack under his arm, heads for home. The halls are quiet. It's dark outside.

Tuesday

The professor leans closer to the computer screen, almost knocking over his coffee cup. Something about the empirical results doesn't look right. He leans back in his chair, closes his eyes, and thinks; he leans forward again, taking another long hard look, frowns, and leans back again. An undergraduate student standing in the hall observes this ritual with some curiosity and wanders away, wondering whether all professors are weird.

The professor spends several hours intensely focused on his screen. He doesn't notice the maintenance person who walks in to check the settings on his phone, or the cleaning person who empties the garbage can. He doesn't even look up when the two students outside his door begin arguing furiously about the outcome of the previous evening's popular reality TV show.

He is finally brought out of his trancelike state when a colleague thumps on his door for the fourth time, shouting his name. With a vacant look, he realizes the colleague is reminding him to come and join the staff meeting, for which he is now five minutes late. He staggers out of his office, muttering something about "Why do we have so many useless meetings?"

As predicted, this is yet another in a long series of meaningless get-togethers. This time the topic of discussion is the possibility the entire department will move into an adjacent building. The chairman points out that this will mean larger offices for most of the faculty, and more space for the graduate students and support staff. Someone blurts out, "The offices are bigger, but everyone knows the air conditioning doesn't work in that building. And the plumbing is even worse!" The chairman winces, and attempts to highlight other praiseworthy aspects of the new building. Some of the faculty are looking out the windows. More senior faculty are shamelessly reading material they brought in with them, completely ignoring the proceedings. *Ah, the benefits of having tenure.*

Later in the afternoon, the professor welcomes his graduate student to the office. He likes working with the students, especially the bright, idealistic, enthusiastic ones. Their naïve curiosity reminds him of himself, half a decade earlier. Life was so much simpler in those early years. You could read articles all day and all night if you wanted, focus on your research and ignore the rest of the world, fantasize about making the next big discovery in the field, and have enough time to fight off the bulge around your waist. He's especially happy to see this graduate student, because she is easily the best student he's ever had. The next few hours don't disappoint. Well-prepared for the meeting, she presents the most recent results of her research, and capably responds to all his efforts to play devil's advocate. Satisfied that she's done a solid job, he says as much. They agree on next steps, and off she goes.

The intellectual stimulation of the encounter leaves him inspired; he quickly closes the door to forestall interruptions, and attacks the manuscript, managing to get far more revision work completed than he could have possibly imagined.

Hours later, feeling good about himself, he answers the phone. It turns out to be the consultant he met a few weeks earlier at a government-sponsored luncheon. The professor sits up a bit straighter when he realizes the caller is wondering whether he'd be interested in some consulting work. Knowing such work is well-compensated, the professor quickly stammers his interest, and the two agree to speak in greater detail early the next week. The professor is so excited he completely forgets the agreed-on time conflicts directly with one of his classes.

Wednesday

The morning begins on an exasperating note; the professor realizes he can't spend more time on his research because there is an urgent request for the faculty to meet the dean for a town hall meeting. He trudges across the university lawn, enters the larger hall; dozens of people are already seated, others are filing in. A few minutes later the dean addresses the gathered crowd. He explains that the state legislature decided the day before to reduce funding for higher education: a public school, the university and the Faculty are very likely to be affected. Regrettably, 20 percent of the hiring for open positions will be frozen. If additional cuts are made, the incoming graduate student classes will likely be downsized. One professor in the front row shouts out with great exasperation, "It's stupid to punish graduate students. Isn't the whole point of the university to create the scholars of the future? This is academic suicide!" The dean, on the defensive, explains there will be other cuts as well. Someone else shouts "You're cutting the graduate students because they don't pay tuition!" The conversation deteriorates from there.

The atmosphere back in the department is subdued. Too depressed to work on more revisions, the professor turns to grading the previous week's assignment. Usually, one of the teaching assistants grades them, but the graduate student's wife had given birth the week before; understandably, he'd been absent ever since. He had called to suggest he could pick the assignments up and try to work on them in the hospital, but the professor assured him the work could be covered by others. He partly regrets that generous gesture, but the monotony of the grading process dulls his senses enough to take the edge off the morning's shocking news.

In the early evening, an undergraduate student knocks lightly on the door. The professor has the vague feeling that the student has sought to see him earlier that week; yes, the student is seeking a recommendation letter for her application to a graduate program. The professor, recognizing one of his best students, quickly agrees, and asks the student to sit down. They speak for about twenty minutes, the professor providing some advice the youngster laps up like a wide-eyed puppy.

Thursday

Once again, it's teaching day. The professor repeats Monday's routine. Once teaching duties are completed, he rushes to the department's meeting room; nodding greetings to gathered colleagues, he takes a seat in the back. This is the weekly seminar series: a PhD student presents his latest research; the event doubles as a practice session for the student, who expects to refine and use this same presentation during his academic job search. While not brilliantly presented, the content is interesting. The professor makes a mental note to speak with the student, thinking he can recommend a few schools that might be good targets for the student's job search.

Immediately after the seminar, the weekly meeting when the department chair takes advantage of the gathering to discuss the news of the day begins; he starts by reminding everyone of the dean's address. Not wanting to make the meeting any longer than needed, no one seems inclined to engage in any discussion. Somewhat surprised at the lack of a strong response, the chairman moves on to another subject. It seems that a nearby college has come under severe scrutiny for allegedly reducing the academic requirements of varsity athletes. The chairman goes on to urge all faculty not to succumb to such prostitution of academic standards. Finally, the chairman calls attention to the spate of cheating incidents, pointing out that the number of academic ethics infractions has been on the rise, and urging all staff members to look for any and all breaches. On that happy note, the meeting breaks up.

Friday

The professor stares, disbelieving, at his computer screen. Somehow, the computer has seized up, destroying the last hour of work. Too exhausted and stunned to verbalize a reaction, he hangs his head, resigned to the loss, taking comfort that most of the revisions made that morning could be reconstructed from notes he'd made the previous evening.

Two hours later, the damage is undone; the professor allows himself a lazy coffee break with two colleagues. The conversation quickly turns from lazy to intense as they come up with a collaborative research idea. Inspired, they go off to their offices, each volunteering to pursue selected tasks which will allow them to gauge the feasibility of the new idea.

While engaged in his subset of tasks, the professor realizes there is a new email message in his inbox, from another journal. He sits, riveted to his chair, reading and hoping for the best, dreading the worst. The email message begins, "I'm delighted to inform you your recent article has been accepted for publication in our journal. Please contact me as soon as possible to discuss administrative details."

Life is good!

Saturday

All day spent in the office, revising.

Sunday

All day spent in the office, revising. One hour catching up with a graduate student.

This hypothetical story is, with minor variations, actually quite typical. The professor may be married, meaning even greater time pressure due to family obligations. Teaching loads vary, depending on the department's available resources and requirements. Young professors also typically have to participate in various committees (recruiting, reviewing applicants for visiting positions, and curriculum overhaul initiatives). Senior faculty members consciously dodge these committee appointments, often regarding them as a serious waste of time.

There are two critical themes in this "week in the life": the first is the overbearing pressure of the tenure decision. The second is the overwhelming dependence of the tenure decision on research (publications) rather than education (teaching). Research nearly always heavily outweighs teaching; even a well-meaning professor's time is redirected under these pressures.

Chapter 2: Preliminary Doctoral Program Requirements

This chapter describes the first phase of the doctoral program—including coursework, laboratory work, comprehensive examinations, and research papers.

Course Work

The typical doctoral program begins with a heavy dose of course work: attending undergraduate-style lectures, although generally in much smaller classes, reading assignments, tests, projects and final exams. Just as there is a significant jump in intensity and difficulty in going from high school to an undergraduate program, PhD-level classes are generally far more challenging than undergraduate courses, leading to quite a shock for many young students. The notion of having to study round-the-clock *just to keep up* is a serious wake-up call, particularly when they come from an institution where easy classes and inflated grades were the norm.

Some programs require candidates to maintain a sufficient grade-point average to remain in good standing, which may have implications for remaining in the program, as well as obtaining or retaining financial support. Incoming students with the weakest backgrounds will generally begin to question their place in the program after just a few weeks, as they feel they are falling further and further behind. Some become so frustrated they withdraw from the program after midterm examinations; due to feelings of embarrassment, they frequently disappear without a word.

Graduate students arrive with very different educational and cultural experiences. Foreign students whose language skills are somewhat lacking may be concerned about committing social *faux pas;* those accustomed to more rigid and hierarchical academic infrastructures may find relaxing enough to thrive in a new environment at least as challenging as the course work.

Not surprisingly, students who are weak across the curriculum may become frustrated with their own (lack of) progress. They are most likely to abandon a program. This is not universally the case, however. There are students who struggle with much of the coursework, yet are able to make the necessary adjustments and perform well on examinations, reestablishing their good standing in the program. Their turnaround is sometimes underlined by the surprising failure of those students who initially seemed to be much better prepared. Both examples are, to a great extent, reflections of people's personalities and levels of commitment.

Challenging course work is just one of the hurdles placed in the path of PhD candidates. Those who can't keep up are identified early on: they can choose to work extra hard to catch up, withdraw from the program and improve their preparation, or drop out altogether. Some have been known to leave for a few months or even a year, acquire or brushup needed skills, then return to the program. While often accompanied by initial embarrassment, this can be a very mature choice. It also highlights the importance of finding out whether one's preparation is sufficient prior to enrollment.

In the grand scheme of graduate work, it's much better for all concerned to find out sooner, rather than later, if a student's preparation is insufficient. A program's published prerequisites are supposed to help incoming students decide whether they have the necessary background, and allow them to prepare appropriately for their entry, but it's impossible to standardize the precise required content. All too frequently, students who believe they meet the prerequisites discover that the advertised list of requirements is inaccurate.

Study Groups

At the graduate level, many students find it helpful to form informal study groups. It is often useful to have someone else to run ideas and thoughts by; collaborating can be very helpful as small mistakes and misunderstandings of the material can be quickly and efficiently corrected. These interactions are useful for developing friendships and feeling more connected within the program and department. Forging strong ties within programs requiring extensive laboratory work (biological and chemical sciences, for example) can be extremely useful, especially when an experiment or procedure requires close supervision and the student is suddenly pulled out of town, finds herself bedridden by disease or injury, or on maternity leave. Knowing that a knowledgeable friend is available to help out with school work can make a very big difference to already-strained morale.

Students with the weakest preparation stand to gain the most from group work early on; they can catch up on material more efficiently and effectively when they have constant access to others who are more knowledgeable. This arrangement can be favorable for the better-prepared students because explaining parts of the material highlights gaps in their own knowledge. A person must know the material to explain it clearly to someone else. Ideally, students studying in groups give and take support, depending on their own strengths and weaknesses.

Some students prefer to work alone: for some, it is simply a personal preference; for others, this choice is a reflection of embarrassment or feelings of inadequacy. Some students drop out of the group and steadily fade away; others work very diligently and catch up outside the group, rejoining later. Yet others are able to withstand the initial embarrassment and stick with the group experience, getting up to speed faster.

Laboratory Work

A lot of learning takes place outside traditional classroom settings. The natural and life sciences fields require much "bench," or laboratory (lab) work; the social sciences may require computer exercises; the visual arts may entail significant studio work, and stage work is a large component for those involved in performance arts. Each of these environments presents particular challenges: thorough preparation prior to enrolling in the graduate program can make a big difference in the student's ultimate success or failure.

Students entering programs requiring lab work often become part of a "family," whose "home" is the laboratory, headed by the principal investigator (PI)—generally the head of the laboratory—who often serves as the students' dissertation advisor. Given the intimate nature of laboratory work, with several students and the PI often crammed together for hours on end, it is critically important for an incoming student to assess the environment ahead of time. A visit (or several) to the laboratory, meetings with other students, and thorough "investigation" of one's potential principal investigator are necessary to evaluate the environment realistically.

Reality Check

After the first semester of course and laboratory work, students often begin to question their decision to join the PhD program. Many stresses, anxieties, and frustrations come in the early months of any graduate program, and nothing has yet been said about comprehensive or preliminary examinations or the dissertation phases: a few months into the program, many students can't face the idea of five more years of the same anxiety.

A reality check is important for at least two reasons. First, it's critical to realize what a graduate program is *not*: it is *not* a return to the jolly old undergraduate life, throwing a Frisbee on the university lawn, painting one's face, screeching at basketball games, and drinking to excess in the campus bar. Second, surviving and completing the program requires many days of monotony, hard work, late nights, disappointments, and frustration. However, it is precisely these lows and challenges that make the successes that much sweeter, that make the spine-tingling excitement at a new discovery so intense, and bring some people tears of joy. One cannot appreciate the meaning of success without experiencing the depths of despair, just as in all aspects of life, not just the academic setting.

It's quite natural to feel intimidated: most graduate students have enjoyed great success in their undergraduate work, often finishing at the top of their class. *Everyone* in graduate programs is very bright, highly motivated, and accustomed to being at the top of the class. Being surrounded for the first time by such intensity and brainpower leads some students to question whether they belong; *every* incoming student questions his adequacy at times, but hardly anyone admits this fact until much later. The key is to work hard and overcome the intimidation.

Some students fall into the trap of continually comparing themselves to others. They want to know everyone's exam and project scores, how long each person worked on a particular assignment, and a whole string of other anxiety-induced tidbits that don't help them progress through the program. Many students assume their colleagues are progressing faster than they are, or that everyone else's dissertation topics are easier and more manageable than their own. These are universal and false beliefs, born of anxiety that fades with maturity.

Comprehensive, Qualifying or Preliminary Examinations

The battery of comprehensive (qualifying or preliminary) examinations, covering significant portions of one's coursework, are frequently a "do or die" program phase. Most doctoral programs have these examination requirements, but in different formats and at different stages of one's studies. They all have several aspects in common: they cover immense amounts of material, last many hours, and preparing for them is extremely stressful. Some exams can, technically, cover any topic ever studied—beginning in kindergarten, and culminating in graduate work. For the record, no one has yet reported a qualifying exam requiring finger painting, or a game of tic-tac-toe, although some programs do require that the candidate play nicely with others.

Some programs set their examinations immediately after the coursework requirement is completed: other programs set examinations later in the program, and students may be responsible for material encountered during their research efforts, in addition to course work.

It's highly advisable to be very organized from day one in the program, mindful that exams can cover any of the materials studied. Students should do the work well ahead of time while progressing through the course and laboratory work, mastering concepts and details continually. There is far too much material to re-read every paper assigned over the previous three years, struggle to piece together class notes, or study from notes written by others and expect to pass exams.

Most students find the prospects of such wide-ranging examinations highly intimidating, even insurmountable. A wise student:

- Maps out a study schedule
- Starts early, often months in advance
- Paces herself to avoid burnout, and
- Treats studying as a full time job, putting in regular, steady hours

The level of satisfaction experienced at completion of each stage of one's PhD program differs, but, unquestionably, the milestones are more joyous and intensely satisfying for those who worked harder and suffered more. The process is also humbling: a student can discover many things about himself, some painful, some encouraging; accepted constructively, this can be a positive, formative stage in one's life.

Preliminary Research Projects

Once the coursework ends, most programs require a research project culminating in a written paper. Some programs consider this paper a formal master's thesis, others do not. This preliminary paper requirement is very useful; it can be a lower-stress exercise than trying to jump directly into the doctoral thesis. Recognizing that the work is a stepping stone to the dissertation—not the dissertation itself—is important. Some programs have no intermediate step, and one moves directly into dissertation research mode.

Best cases allow preliminary research to eventually lead to a final thesis, but, often, a student can be satisfied if the work leads to even a minor publication. Viewing preliminary research and paper-writing as a useful opportunity to learn the ropes of academia—undertaking research, presenting one's results and learning how to accept feedback graciously and analyze criticisms correctly—is one excellent way to test the academic waters.

Perhaps, for the first time in his graduate-school career, a student will now engage in actual research. *Finally*, he will do what academics actually busy themselves doing for the balance of their careers: focus on a particular problem, read the relevant literature—journal articles, conference proceedings, text books, perhaps unpublished manuscripts or notebooks from historic archives. He may write computer code or sit down and solve mathematical equations and models; he may travel extensively and undertake field work. He may begin to cultivate cultures, viruses, or breed animals.

Sometimes, it's very odd for students to suddenly be doing actual research. After sixteen to eighteen years of traditional in-class course work, this is, frequently, the first time they experience the intensity of real research. Some (in fact, many) lose their orientation. Suddenly, without structure imposed by a teacher—no class notes, obvious reading lists, or textbooks outlining that day's material with test questions at the end of each chapter—it's as if the rug has been pulled out from under their feet. "What do I do now?" is a frequent silent (or not-so-silent) question.

As the weeks and months go by in any program, the pressure on a student to articulate a dissertation idea that is innovative, original, and acceptable to one's dissertation committee increases steadily. Resisting this self-imposed anxiety in the early stages of research is wise. Ideally, a less-ambitious first project is a lower-stress opportunity to learn the process of doing research, and master the mental and physical discipline that will serve the student well in future years. A smaller project is more manageable, yields results sooner, and a first success helps build self-confidence.

Occasionally, the initial paper will lead her on a (usually winding) thread to the ultimate dissertation topic, or the student may ultimately decide to pursue something very different for her dissertation.

Throughout this process, it is necessary and useful to seek guidance from any professors willing to provide feedback. If the student hasn't already done so, this stage of a program is a good time to begin evaluating potential dissertation advisors.

Research Assistantships

Some students undertake research as research assistants, supporting a more senior professor in her research, rather than embarking independently on their own. Research assistantships are required in some programs, often qualifying the student for financial support or tuition waivers. The assistantship is not required in other programs, but provides some income. The real benefits of a research assistantship are not merely financial, however: the opportunity to work closely with an established professor has great educational benefit, and offers a chance to get to know at least one faculty member well. The relationship can lead to valuable mentoring, identifying a future dissertation advisor or dissertation committee member, and access to the established academic's networks for job offers and recommendations.

Presenting Research

As soon as the student begins research, regardless of the stage of the doctoral program, she must begin thinking about presenting her research to others. The best way to learn how to present one's work is to practice in front of an audience, informally or formally.

Informal presentations are typically delivered in seminars and workshops, to fellow students, or a small, informal gathering of professors. Some students organize their own casual forums. Young professors often join students at these events as a way of participating and connecting with recent arrivals to the program. Casual forums encourage lighthearted discussions, making personal connections, and are ideal opportunities for practicing and improving presentation skills. The material presented need not be highly polished; some allow videotaping, an ideal way to examine one's own performance from the audience's perspective.

Formal presentations are delivered at conferences, as well as during events within one's own school or when visiting other schools; one presents polished work, generally to an audience of faculty members. Understandably, these presentations can be far more stressful than informal forums, but also promise greater rewards in terms of personal development: the more intense the setting, the greater the potential for learning. Formal events are also opportunities to network with other researchers, get very important feedback on one's work, learn the interests of others, get a feel for the bigger picture, and find like-minded individuals who may become collaborators, friends, and future colleagues.

Formal or informal, any presentation is an opportunity for getting professional feedback and developing presentation skills. The importance of presentation skills cannot be overemphasized: a student must "sell" her research results to a variety of audiences. One can read and take classes to improve pronunciation and vocabulary, practice presentations alone in a room or in front of a mirror. But, there is no substitute for the experience of facing an audience! Do not waste these opportunities, even if the setting is informal. Think about physical posture, gestures, intonations for variety and emphasis, facial expressions—do they enhance or detract from your message clarity? Are your audiovisual tools and presentation materials excellent? Do you know how to use them effectively and unobtrusively? Using slides or overheads that can't be easily read or understood is a cardinal sin: furthermore, flashy audiovisuals may be frowned upon, because some academics have a deep-rooted suspicion that glitz and flash are used to obscure lack of meaningful content in a presentation.

Standing up and speaking in public is an intimidating proposition for most people, but it's necessary. Many gain tremendous confidence, and find public presentations exhilarating. Some always suffer some stage fright. Reducing some of the intimidation at presenting in a new place can be as simple as a reconnaissance mission—visit the presentation hall, walk around and size the place up, practice some or all of the presentation in the actual location. When it's time for the real show, the setting is familiar and, therefore, less intimidating.

The more confident the presenter, the more effective his message. Brilliant research doesn't sell itself, and can be overshadowed by the work of lesser talents with more extroverted personalities. Talent is important in the ivory tower—but, as in all other aspects of life—success is closely linked to marketing. A presenter must maximize the positive exposure: a talk must be well-reasoned, well-written, and well-rehearsed, in as realistic a set of conditions as possible. During practice sessions, solicit feedback on the content, clarity of your message, and the professionalism of your appearance and delivery. Arguments must have substance. Weaknesses must be understood and, to the extent possible, associated criticism anticipated and defensible responses formulated and weighed in advance.

Using *performance* and *show* to describe your presentation does not imply that it is a façade: quite the opposite, in fact. The substance must be presented professionally for maximum impact. Professional presenters are well-prepared, adhere to time limits out of respect for the audience's other obligations, and deliver real content in a comfortable and, as appropriate, even entertaining fashion.

Professional presenters seek a pace or rhythm and select their material carefully: they always leave enough time to share their most important results, leaving out unnecessary details. Many inexperienced presenters forget to budget time for audience questions or allow themselves to become engaged in tangential discussions. Subsequently, they run out of time before delivering their punch line.

Depending on the field of study, students may also need to work on their poster presentation skills. While it may be more prestigious to secure a speaking engagement at a conference, it is typically easier to gain exposure by presenting a poster (described later in this book). Posters are lower-stress opportunities to write up results and discuss them in relatively informal settings with people who express interest as they walk through a convention hall. These one-on-one or one-on-several sessions afford multiple opportunities to obtain feedback on one's research, as well as engage in networking.

Writing Papers and Submitting to Journals

A scholar shares her research ideas and results primarily through the written word, most often in the form of manuscripts submitted to journals for publication. The key is to do thorough research, present it to best effect by putting together a high-quality manuscript: a clearly explained argument is more powerful and appealing and makes the reader's and reviewer's jobs easier. Those who do not communicate well in writing are at a distinct disadvantage. Many highly intelligent people fail to reach their full academic potential because they lack these critical, learned skills: important contributions are stifled because they are not presented in the best light.

One can actually *learn* how to write cogently and persuasively, so students need not panic if they find articulating thoughts on paper difficult at first. Reading widely and making the effort to understand the structure and flow of a good paper in one's field is excellent practice in both writing and research. Fortunately, word processing programs lend themselves to the editing and revising process, and can be used to fix grammar and spelling mistakes.

Reviewers always have too many papers to read: every day, they must make quick decisions about which papers they will read and which will be set aside. The author is obligated to make her paper user-friendly and as readable as possible, to be clear about the theory, the data, the empirical analyses, and most important—the results and their interpretation.

You should distribute drafts and solicit feedback from others; members of one's own faculty and colleagues at other institutions are good resources. There are usually some very keen and capable graduate students who will eagerly read other students' papers; however, an established professor's experience in the field and knowledge of editorial board preferences will prove highly instructive. Be mindful, at all times, that readers volunteer their scarce time to review your work; do not overburden them with a new version every week. Alternating readers can help reduce inconvenience for any one person, and yields a broader feedback set.

In a given field, hundreds or thousands of new papers may be written each year! It's physically impossible for anyone to read each and every article written in her field; the academic community has embraced a convention of abstracts (described later in this book), which serve as executive summaries. As soon as the graduate student begins writing, she must also begin practicing the art of the written abstract; succinctly summarizing the essence of her paper and making the reader hungry for more.

Grant Writing

Grants are the major source of funding for laboratories and students, and, in some cases, professors' salaries. Grants are not relevant in all fields, but are ubiquitous in the life and hard sciences.

Grants come from government sources, private foundations, and sponsoring corporations, and generally do not have to be repaid, as would a loan. Competing for and winning grants takes special skill and perseverance; anyone skilled at generating grant money is prized in an academic department, because money rules! Money funds laboratory assistants, buys computers, other equipment and materials, pays travel expenses, provides job security and leads to prestige and even more grants.

Occasionally, good grant writers are taken advantage of by others. For example, an advisor may not allow a student to complete his PhD in a timely fashion because it's very useful to have him around longer, helping with grant applications. Despite this potential downside, the ability to write a solid grant application or proposal is a very good thing, and will help secure a good employment position when the time comes. Since money speaks so loudly, it's possible for a less-talented researcher to obtain a better academic appointment than a more-talented applicant if the former is better at generating research funds.

Teaching Assistantships

It's quite common in most programs for graduate students to assist professors' classroom efforts. Depending upon the program, one may work alongside the advisor; in others, one may find employment with other members of the faculty.

Graduate students in their early years may be restricted to grading papers and answering basic questions, but, over time, duties may include leading laboratory sessions or full-fledged teaching duties.

Teaching assistantships are not always required, although they are a good source of income for graduate students. Some students prefer to spend their time on research; however, gaining some teaching experience early in one's career is valuable, because such skills will eventually be required in an academic career. The act of teaching also forces the instructor to practice delivering her message more clearly to others, which directly improves presentation skills.

Chapter 3: The Dissertation

The best-known, and often most daunting, element of a doctoral program is the doctoral dissertation. The formal requirement is that a dissertation must be "a unique and significant contribution to society's collective knowledge."

This chapter addresses the roles of the advisor and dissertation committee, the dissertation proposal, the dissertation, and its defense.

The Dissertation Advisor

Undeniably (in addition to the student himself), the most important player in the PhD student's academic arena is the dissertation committee chair. This person is responsible for guiding the student throughout the program, and assisting in her training and development. In some fields this person may be referred to as the advisor, mentor, committee chair, or principal investigator (PI). The latter is commonly used in the life sciences where one's studies take place within a laboratory environment. By default, this book uses the generic term "advisor," although wherever especially relevant, "principal investigator" may be used for clarity.

An academic graduate program is considered a full-time job; the advisor is essentially the boss. This boss comes into the picture at different stages of the program, depending on the school and field of study. Selection of the dissertation committee advisor may come as late as the second or third year of some programs; in others, one's admission to the graduate program is specifically geared to working with a pre-identified person.

As a rule, upon gaining entry into a program, one should immediately begin looking for and considering potential advisors. If at all possible, some investigation should be undertaken ahead of time to identify potential advisor candidates before, or during, the application to the school.

The advisor doesn't need to be a friend, although, in many cases, very strong relationships do develop. Sometimes, the relationship is a more distant, mentor-student arrangement. There is nothing wrong with either, so long as both parties are professional, constructive, and productive.

Some relationships are sour from the beginning, not good for anyone; such pairings usually fall apart. In the more favorable "divorce" cases, the now older and wiser student is able to find a better match and succeeds in the program. In the harshest scenarios, the student leaves the program empty-handed. Note the use of the word *harshest* here, rather than *worst*. The distinction is important: some students don't belong in the program, and the falling-out is a natural consequence of an insufficiently motivated student, or one who lacks some critical skills he is unable or unwilling to acquire. In such cases, withdrawal from the program is harsh, but, in the long run, a good outcome for all concerned because the ex-student can move on to explore a more productive future elsewhere, and the advisor is free to spend more time with more appropriate candidates.

In some cases, the separation results from changed circumstances: a professor may take an extended leave or be denied tenure. In either case, an insurmountable geographic distance may force students to seek a different advisor.

In other cases, the relationship suffers because the advisor is not cut out to be a good mentor or boss. Advisors can be self-centered, domineering, and/or treat students as "hired help" or second-class citizens. Such advisors don't help develop a student's skills, waste time, sap emotional energy, and may become an insurmountable obstacle to the ultimate goal—successful thesis defense.

Clearly, careful selection of one's advisor is critical. Students who neglect to keep this in mind when selecting their advisor frequently suffer, switching advisors (or laboratories and PIs) in midstream, or dropping out of the program. Switching advisors isn't a guaranteed option, and must not be relied upon. Furthermore, the very need to switch advisors may be interpreted by some in the academic community as a negative; it raises concerns that the student can't get along with other people. Given the superior/dependent relationship, the onus on making the relationship work is on the student, as the advisor has little incentive to adjust his or her behavior in the near-term.

All else being equal, a student should strive to secure the most senior person possible as her advisor, because a more established mentor's name will carry more weight in grant applications, publication submissions, and employment searches.

How does one go about that selection process? There are two typical scenarios: first, the student is in the graduate program for a year or two before having to make the decision. Second, the advisor or PI is identified prior to one's application to the program.

Seeking an Advisor After a Few Years in the Program

In the first case, the student has the time to get to know the department's faculty members, gauge the important professional characteristics each professor brings to the table, and assess the potential for personal rapport in a prospective relationship.

A common mistake is leaving the search for "later." Students should begin filtering candidates for this critical pairing on day one. Most programs begin with a heavy dose of classroom instruction; each course is a convenient forum for getting to know a faculty member. One course may be taught by several professors, giving each student an excellent opportunity to compare several faculty members' classroom manners, preparation, and passion for the subject.

Students should go to as many department functions as possible; weekly or monthly social gatherings can be great for breaking the ice and realizing that professors can be Nobel laureates *and* approachable, fun, and friendly. Seminar presentations are important for gauging a professor's incisiveness, level of interest, and respect for others' work. During a seminar, students seeking advisors should focus on a professor and ask themselves:

- Does he participate in the seminar discussions or just sit back and not appear to really care?
- Does he make an effort to understand other people's work, or does he care only about his own?
- Does he comment constructively, or does he relish embarrassing others and establishing himself as the "smartest" person in the room?

All aforementioned interactions (classrooms, departmental functions, seminars, one-on-one conversations) are useful for investigating an advisor candidate's critical characteristics:

- Do the professor's students ultimately obtain good work positions, or do they struggle?
- Is there any reason to be concerned about the professor's ethical standards and practices?
- Does the professor respect students? Mutual respect is a critical requirement for a constructive relationship.
- Will the professor give credit for discoveries and findings to others? Does he always insist on being First Author? Is credit shared fairly among teammates?
- Does the professor write good reference letters for students seeking employment?
- Will the professor provide useful answers to questions? Feedback on paper drafts should be meaningful and constructive, rather than destructive.

- Will the professor provide timely feedback on a student's work? Is guidance on a student's planned research, fieldwork, or studies forthcoming? If not, progress may be delayed.

- Will the professor have reasonable expectations for the student? Good advisors demand diligence and intellectual rigor, pushing students to achieve, but their demands are realistic and accompanied with supportive suggestions.

- Is the professor approachable and available? Does he keep appointments and remain "present" for his students? A professor who is always very busy may be difficult to find.

- Is the professor amenable to joint work with his students, or does he insist on publishing his own papers separately?

- How is the professor's work funded? Is there a reasonable guarantee funding will continue steadily or a possibility funding will end? If funding sources are external entities such as private corporations, are there any implications for patents or copyright that impact the advisor, and, potentially, the student and his work?

- Will the professor help the student obtain funding? The advisor may be happy to have the student as a resource, but is he willing to help the student as well? This trait separates the truly supportive advisors from those who are indifferent or ineffectual.

- Does the professor care about his students personally or is he like an automaton going through the motions, insensible, or simply unable to relate to others? An advisor who is a good human being makes life much more enjoyable, and getting through the program easier and more fulfilling for the student.

- Is the professor committed to the students' development? Is his mentoring sound, and unselfish? Does he arrange or extend opportunities to attend, and present at, conferences?

- Does the professor have constructive relationships with other members of the faculty? If not, why not? Students who affiliate themselves with a professor shunned by much of the faculty may put their own work and reputation at risk.

- Is the professor passionate about his teaching? Does he get excited about the subject matter? Good classroom teachers and people who take pride in their in-class performance are frequently those who will have the inclination and patience to be good teachers in one-on-one student-advisor relationships.

- Is the professor tenured, and/or will he be around long enough to take his students through completion of their program? If his tenure is denied, it is almost a certainty the professor will leave the institution. An advisor's premature departure can significantly disrupt a student's work.

- How many students does the professor have? Many students can be a good signal, but this can also mean less time available to nurture any one student. Furthermore, some professors like having students around simply because they are cheap, obedient labor or entitle their professor to more departmental funding.

- Does the professor have the students' best interests at heart? Is he loyal to them? Loyalty is critical because there may be future situations when the professor will need to speak up on their behalf.

- Do the professor's students amass a respectable number of publications during the course of the doctoral program? (This may not be realistic in all programs.)

- How long do the professor's students take to complete their studies? It's a strong positive signal if students graduate on schedule; and a strong negative signal if they take much longer than the average.

- How frequently do the professor's students fail to graduate? A higher-than-average failure rate is a very negative signal. Are there any characteristics common to students who fail to graduate, suggesting biases or prejudices on the professor's part?

- Is the professor well established and respected in his field? Reputation translates into having good connections and more clout in helping students obtain good positions after graduation; a disgraced professor's reputation may cast a shadow on a student's career and limit academic and employment opportunities.

- Does the professor have many external interests, such as consulting? Outside engagements may mean lower priority assigned to students, and less accessibility. Advisors who spend a lot of time on external interests may also be a bit out of touch with recent research.

- Is the professor technically sharp and an expert in the field of interest? The professor needn't be the world's expert in the student's particular field of interest, but his knowledge must be sufficient to provide solid guidance, call attention to important papers in the field, and help the student avoid wasting time.

Very few professors will display all these qualities; a larger, more diverse dissertation committee can supplement a single advisor's expertise and available time.

A useful way to begin a relationship with a professor is through research or teaching assistantships. Some schools assign graduate students as assistants, but it's usually possible to have at least some input into the process, especially after the first semester or year. Approaching a professor personally, stating interest in the professor's work, suggesting the possibility of becoming an assistant is a first step in evaluating him as an advisor; gauge his initial reaction carefully. If the reaction is cool or negative, it's time to move on and seek a relationship with a different professor. If the reaction is favorable, one can proceed to build a stronger relationship. After a time, some students find the match isn't as good as they'd hoped; they should repeat the initial process with someone else. Some students are rightfully concerned that leaving that first relationship will send a bad signal—all the more reason to begin carefully and not commit until both sides are comfortable. In all cases, it's important to be open, honest, and respectful.

Identifying an Advisor Prior to Entering the Program

Some graduate programs require immediate advisor identification. It's clearly more difficult to gauge answers to the questions listed above, unless there is an opportunity to interact with the potential advisor prior to applying to the program. Students who've recently completed undergraduate work in the same institution may have an advantage as they will (ideally) have already developed relationships. However, most students don't have the benefit of such proximity to a prospective advisor because it's generally recommended that students pursue graduate studies in a different institution than their undergraduate one.

Still, students can gauge potential advisors from afar. Specifically, students can (and obviously should) read a prospective advisor's papers, and investigate her standing within the academic community. Discussing her performance with other students who know the professor can be critically important. If laboratory work is involved, communicating with other members of that laboratory is a must, as in these cases the student will be joining an entire academic "family" rather than one professor. Positive rapport with other team or family members will make life much easier, and could make the difference between success and failure in the program.

Listen to your own instincts during and after communicating with a professor (and, if necessary, members of the laboratory). Was there a good "vibe" from these people? Is the prospect of spending several years with them appealing, or unappealing? *This is the time to be picky!* Far too many students, after many years of hard work, lament that, had they known what their advisor (or the environment) was really like, they would have gone elsewhere, or would not have pursued the PhD at all. Allowing for some harmless whining by students voicing such thoughts, it should be clear that making a good decision about one's advisor is more than half the distance on the road to a doctoral degree.

Limit to the Advisor's Power

Dissertation advisors have tremendous influence on, and power over, their students in all fields, but nowhere more so than in laboratory settings. This section focuses on the most powerful advisors—the principal investigators (PIs).

All graduate students (masters and PhDs) and postdoctoral fellows (described in greater detail in a later chapter) within a lab are employed by the PI. The underlings in this "family" structure are much more likely to (not so jokingly) refer to this person as "God" than "father" or "mother," because their fate is entirely in the PI's hands. The PI determines who does what around the lab, who participates in which specific studies, who gets credit, who is ready to present research results in conferences, etc., and, of course, whether one is ready to graduate and move on. The PI's recommendations and efforts in the job-search phase are critical in helping the graduating student find a good position as a faculty member or postdoctoral fellow. The PI is comparable to the dissertation committee advisor in other fields, but the relationship with the students is much closer (in time and physical proximity) because everything revolves around the laboratory and its functions.

Does the PI or advisor have *unlimited* power over the student? Of course not! Abusive behavior such as intimidation and harassment is clearly unacceptable; so are more subtle abuses of power, such as having a student dog- or house-sit for a professor. When the professor-student interaction has moved to genuine two-way friendship, such requests wouldn't raise eyebrows; absent mutual regard and friendship, however, such requests could be considered abusive and inappropriate.

Whether a professor's behavior is criminal, illegal, or merely inappropriate, students do have recourse through department chairs, ombudsmen, and other on-campus resources to restrain an advisor's unreasonable behavior or demands. Often, however, students are reluctant to take formal actions due to concerns about potential retaliation by the professor in question. Thus, rather than confront the advisor, minor annoyances are frequently overlooked. This imbalance of power (in favor of the professor) places the student in a precarious position. Sadly, some professors do abuse that power.

The line between appropriate and inappropriate can be relative to a society's norms. Going beyond North America's shores, one may observe very different, and more readily accepted, power-wielding by senior professors. Consider the following example of a professor I met in Japan. He was a fairly meek fellow at home where he lived under the shadow of his rather intimidating wife. As she ran the household with an iron fist, he preferred spending long hours on campus, frequently sleeping in his office. Unlike the situation at home, where he would be put in his place by a domineering wife, in his office he was undisputed king, with a half-dozen students (masters and PhDs) at his beck and call 24 hours a day. The students did everything for him, from continually making tea, making his bed, washing the dishes in his office to serving his guests. Frequently, he would declare that they were all going out, forcing them all to join him at a bar and drink with him; there was never a thought they could leave early to attend to outstanding work or family obligations. If he stayed late in the office, they were obligated to stay as long as he did; when he stayed overnight, they were compelled to stay until the wee hours of the morning. At least one of them (always one of the women living on campus) would then have to wake up at 5 AM to make his breakfast. It's impossible to imagine any North American student agreeing to this level of servitude, or any North American university tolerating it. Yet, his behavior and the students' acquiescence were not out of line within the boundaries of local culture.

Boundaries on Advisor-Student Relationships

The controversial issue of advisor-student dating must be addressed. Professors dating students at the same university raise propriety and legal issues, magnified a hundredfold when the professor is also the student's advisor.

In the worst cases, a professor takes advantage of his power to exert outright illegal influence. Professors have been known to intimidate students, tying classroom success to sexual favors. These are very serious issues; good schools explain the proprieties of professor-student relationships during student orientation periods, and identify on-campus resources to deal with inappropriate and/or unwanted attention. Students are wise to make note of these resources (and hope they'll never be needed).

While extreme forms of abuse are infrequent, there is no foolproof system that protects against all such eventualities. Furthermore, there are frequently legally gray areas around consensual-versus-manipulated relationships. Many universities go the ultraconservative route by imposing very explicit and broad nonfraternization rules on professors to avoid creating even the perception of wrongdoing. The safest solution for both students and professors is not to get romantically involved with each other. The onus is on the professor, who is in the more powerful position, to adhere to appropriate standards of behavior.

These conservative rules are not accepted by all; some students and professors argue that such policies are Draconian, asserting that an academic field of study brings together like-minded people, and it's natural for them to have mutual admiration and attraction. Given the inherent seclusion in academic life, they believe excluding those candidates most attractive to them from intimate consideration is unfair and unrealistic. This argument goes on to say that graduate students are adult enough to take care of themselves and that administrators shouldn't interfere with their personal lives.

Student/professor fraternization has long been, and will continue to be, a contentious subject. Abuse of a relationship may be very infrequent, but a university must set policies and take action that protects against those few occurrences.

Dissertation Committee

The dissertation committee is responsible, under the leadership of the advisor or committee chair, for providing support, advice, and guidance to the student throughout the dissertation stage. The members of this committee form the panel responsible for periodically evaluating student performance, conducting the final oral examination, and final confirmation that the dissertation meets an appropriately high standard of scholarship to justify graduation.

The structure of these committees and their practical functions vary significantly across institutions and departments. Thus, the level of involvement of the various committee members may differ widely.

To create the most supportive committee, a student should think carefully about the skills each member has to offer. The objective is to structure a team which covers the traits, skills and contacts that best serve his needs. In some sense, a committee is selected to buttress or complement the skills and connections of the advisor. No student has complete freedom in selecting this committee. Choices must conform to the department's guidelines, and are constrained to the list of faculty members who are able and willing to participate.

Students should seek committee members who have:

- Good academic contacts, to help with finding academic employment and future collaborators
- Superior knowledge in the relevant field, to set the stage for the student to also become a recognized expert in the field
- Very good intuition and vision, to ensure that research is relevant within the context of efforts by others in the field
- Good industry contacts, to help with research funding and eventual employment
- Very good technical skills, to enable them to spot and correct any significant student errors
- Time and availability to discuss progress consistently; committee members may or may not be as directly involved as the advisor, but it is very useful if they are accessible when needed
- Prestige. Working with a famous scientist can endow the student with an important pedigree to accompany her for the rest of her career
- Established credentials for obtaining funding to support ongoing research; since, in some fields, little can be undertaken

without funding, alliances with people who can attract money are critical

Typical committees number three to five members, and may be subject to the requirement that at least one represent a different department, or even faculty, within the school. Small schools may sometimes require that one member be from another university entirely. At least some, and sometimes all, committee members must be full professors; adjunct or emeritus professors may be eligible for membership.

Changing a committee's composition midstream is uncommon, but may be permitted depending on each school's rules. Such changes must be approved by the committee chair, and sometimes, even by the department chair or dean.

Dissertation Proposal

Before embarking on the dissertation project, a student is typically required to submit a proposal outlining the intended course of research. The student may actually have to defend this proposal before other faculty members; the logic is that the student, her advisor, and the entire committee are about to commit time and money to this effort, so the student is obligated to prove that the proposed project is worthy of everyone's time.

The proposal can be thought of as a "contract" between the student and his advisor. "I, the student, pledge to undertake the following research in an effort to investigate the following academic question. Once I've completed the outlined tasks, I will have qualified for the PhD, which the faculty will duly grant me." It's acceptable to change the proposal or contract, but changes should be clearly understood by, and acceptable to, all parties.

An acceptable dissertation can be based on formulation of a new theory, research methodology, technique, empirical result, or discovery of new data for empirical research—emphasis on the word "new." The project must address a meaningful problem and must tie into other known results in the collective literature. Dissertations should add a building block to society's knowledge in a particular field.

The proposal defense may, or may not, play a prominent formal role in a particular program; it is only a formality in some, but may be a strict and highly involved process in others. It's advisable, of course, to formulate a dissertation idea over several months—possibly years—before the proposal defense date. When that date comes, the student has already completed preliminary research and had meaningful discussions with her advisor and others regarding the merits of the proposal.

The student should have an advisor by the proposal phase, but, depending on the program, may or may not already have a full committee selected. A successful proposal defense will help a student select committee members from the audience of faculty members. With or without a full committee, the advisor's guidance is critical: her recommendations should shape the proposal, ensuring it explores a meaningful issue, and that the exploration can be completed in timely fashion, with the resources on hand.

A student often feels out of his depth as he gazes across a room at inquisitive, even skeptical, faces poised to challenge his proposal. Ideally, the buildup to this event has forced the student to think objectively and crystallize his thoughts. It's acceptable at this stage to have some outstanding unknowns, as much of the investigation has yet to be undertaken. The student is responsible, however, for proving that he understands the frame of reference and how his selected topic adds new insights and connections in the broader picture. Some proposal outlines are quite general, while others are very detailed, depending on the program and the advisor. The process is informal in some schools, quite formal in others. It is always best to err on the side of formality if there is any doubt.

Here's one dissertation-related horror story, albeit with a happy ending for the student. A political science student had completed all coursework and examinations in his PhD program. He prepared a highly specific dissertation proposal and submitted it to two faculty members who'd agreed to be his joint thesis advisors. Both signed off on his proposal, and both provided him with some feedback along the way. Two years later, the student submitted the completed product. One professor responded with a surprising list of criticisms of the approach taken: it was painfully clear the professor hadn't paid much attention to the proposal, and had never fully read earlier drafts of the dissertation.

The student was outraged and took the matter to the dean. The case was ultimately escalated to the university president; the thesis was approved. The professor in question was dismissed from his post.

This outcome is rare. Such a clear victory for a student is highly atypical in the academic world. Going over a professor's head generally causes damage to the student, even when she is in the right. Protect yourself by getting everyone on board with your ideas, and be the one who ensures there is consensus on your research plan, deadlines for progress mileposts or benchmarks, and a clear working definition of "completion." Some students work on and on for years, and take forever to formally complete their work because no concrete benchmark for completion was established earlier in the process.

Early in the process, a student may consider several legitimate dissertation topics, and wonder which to pursue. It's impossible to tell which research idea will be successful, or whether any one of the choices will bear fruit. Months, even years, may be spent chasing down an idea only to eventually discover it doesn't work, isn't solvable, or is too small an issue to qualify as a dissertation topic. Rather than wait endlessly for some divine signal as to which idea is the perfect one, it's advisable to pick one and pursue it for a while. Within a few months, the student, or at least her advisor, should have an idea of whether this path has the potential to lead to a constructive end. If not, a student can still easily change direction early in the process: time already spent usually proves to be a useful learning experience, so one need not be concerned that time has been wasted. The alternative to choosing an idea and moving forward is procrastinating—doing nothing, truly wasting time without any real benefits. Choosing to do nothing for a time does not guarantee that a perfect dissertation will magically materialize.

Choosing the dissertation topic is, for most people, a gradual process; many students finally defend a dissertation very different from the paper envisioned just a year or two earlier. Recognize that research is exploration; the whole purpose of study and exploration is knowledge. Ideas change, coalesce, mutate in unexpected ways—the mystery makes research exciting, so remain flexible and embrace outcomes you didn't anticipate. Don't burden yourself with self-imposed pressure to move a mountain that can't be moved, or to stubbornly seek a mountain which doesn't exist. Mastering a body of knowledge can be frustrating, with many emotional peaks and valleys, but as long as you continue to read, keep track of the bigger picture, and discuss your ideas with a wide audience, you will ultimately arrive at a problem both meaningful and manageable.

Undertaking Dissertation Research and Writing the Dissertation

Once the dissertation proposal hurdle has been cleared, it's time to make the world a better place. Unique idea in hand, the student embarks on the most challenging stage of his career. The student also has a new title—All But Dissertation (ABD). Some schools bestow the title "candidate"; as the names imply, the student has completed all requirements with the exception of the final dissertation and is a legitimate candidate for the doctoral degree. But that final step is far from automatic. In fact, for this final stage of the PhD program, all semblance of structure disappears. The need to make her unique contribution means she must go where no one has gone before in the vastness of human intellectual pursuit. Some liken the final stages to being thrown to the wolves with only wits, temperament, and commitment to rely on. The greatest challenge begins.

Some points to keep in mind: the dissertation is the *beginning* of a career, and need not be a Nobel prize-winning effort. It is important to maintain balance between being, as a new PhD, *an* expert in her chosen field versus expecting, given the level of specialization required these days, to be, as some would say the graduate should, by definition, be *the* expert in her field. The student should challenge herself to identify and articulate important questions and seek to answer them, but she must also avoid an overly complex proposal: a research project can open up into a huge and unmanageable challenge.

Several decades ago, a typical thesis was many hundreds of pages, and, quite often, a rambling discourse. The usual joke was that no one actually *read* these, and certainly not the dissertation committee. People who wanted to make the point that reading material was very boring would say it was "as dry as a doctoral dissertation."

The painfully long dissertation is still a fixture in some fields; in others, the style has shifted dramatically. Recognition that doctoral theses will ultimately be converted into smaller, article-length submissions to journals led to a sensible evolution: many dissertations are now typically composed of three distinct chapters, each readily convertible into an article. Moving from one continuous, lengthy document also simplifies the thesis work: treating elements of the problem separately, whether a common thread runs through the components or there is no apparent connection, brings the long discourse under control. Once a sufficient number of fragments are written, they can be compiled into one volume which meets the final dissertation requirement. The length and structure of the dissertation depends on one's program; the advisor must make it clear (well in advance) what she considers acceptable.

There are many ups and downs in this research voyage; exaltation at some significant breakthrough can be quickly replaced by the agony of disappointing results. When the data and the words are falling into place, one feels on top of the world and confidence soars. The student feels ready to challenge the experts to open debates. When the puzzle pieces just don't fit, or contradict, devastation follows; a student can easily convince herself she doesn't deserve to be at school, that she's a loser and a fool. The roller-coaster ride continues for two, three, or even four years—as the months and years pass, the peaks seem very fleeting while the valleys are long and depressing. One has to dig deep inside one's own soul, searching for the will to climb out of the valley; personal passion, deeply rooted, centers the mind, enabling the thick-skinned stubbornness necessary to completing the journey. Giving up without completing the dissertation often means carrying the emotional scars of failure forever. Success means taking one's place among the few who've weathered the storms, and earned the coveted PhD.

What is the worst thing that can happen? The following may not be the worst in the grand scheme of things, but it's prominent among doctoral candidates' nightmares. After several months or years of dissertation work, the student comes to the devastating realization that someone has already discovered the idea and published it. Dissertations must be *unique* and *original*. If the work, regardless of how much time has been spent on it, was merely a repetition of someone else's, it does not qualify, deflating the student emotionally; some students are so completely devastated they are unable to face repeating the process with different research, and drop out of school. In some cases this happens after four or five years in the program! But, in most cases, not all is lost. One can re-orient the work and make it still qualify for a dissertation, utilizing some of the earlier work. Nevertheless, re-orienting a dissertation after expending months and years of time and energy can be very demoralizing.

Failure to realize one's work is unoriginal is a cardinal sin, especially in this day and age of the Internet and electronic communications, which allow everyone to search through evidence of existing research far more easily than in the past. The onus for ensuring this doesn't happen is on the student, but, to a lesser degree, on the dissertation advisor. The *student* is ultimately responsible for searching the existing literature and ensuring his work is unique; the advisor's job is to provide more experienced guidance, and, at the very least, help shape and direct the search.

When the student's research is in line with the advisor's—a common situation—the advisor should be intimately familiar with the field and all relevant existing literature. When the student's work is significantly different from the professor's, the professor should be responsible enough to direct the student to other faculty members who may be more knowledgeable in the field, or even to faculty members in different universities.

The advisor must also weigh-in if the topic is too adventurous or innovative: the student may be fascinated by a research idea, only to find that the traditional research community doesn't share this appreciation. The advisor is in a better position to recognize the potential difficulties for revolutionary ideas, and must relay this to the student. Yes, there are examples of going against the grain and being proven correct. More frequently, however, such efforts lead to prolonged debates and cost a lot of precious time. Granted, the very essence of academics should be to rock the boat and challenge traditional views; however, it's sometimes more politically astute to postpone the revolutionary ideas until after graduation.

Finally, the advisor must ensure the dissertation work is attributable to the student alone. This is most relevant in fields where collaborative work is the norm, because, for the purpose of the dissertation, collaboration is not acceptable. The student's work must be sufficiently separate from other activities and individuals to ensure there is no doubt about who has performed the work and to whom credit is due.

Defending the Dissertation

Upon completion of the dissertation, the candidate submits the work to the dissertation committee. This is almost always followed by the last battle of the PhD process—oral defense of the work. Once the oral defense is completed, the committee, headed by its chair, pronounces judgment with one of several possible outcomes. The most devastating, and most infrequent, is an outright "Fail." This is a catastrophic outcome, which essentially says "Back to the drawing board," or "Go home!" On the rare occasions when a student presents his defense and fails, one must consider the advisor's role—the advisor's responsibility is to ensure a student is ready to go before the committee. The student's failure may be as much the professor's failure as his own. Sometimes students insist on moving to the evaluation stage despite warnings from the advisor, making a fail grade more likely.

"Pass, with revisions required" is a much more common outcome; the student has completed the defense requirements, but must revise the work before final submission. The dissertation committee members sign off on the dissertation, the student makes the necessary changes (taking two to six months, on average), and simply shows the revised work to the committee chair for final approval.

The most welcome result is "Pass, with minor or no revisions." Requiring no revisions at all is relatively infrequent: having some minor changes required, taking two months or less to incorporate, is more typical. The committee chair signs off on the dissertation.

The dissertation defense process varies significantly across fields of study and cultures. Within North America alone, there are very different structures to the oral dissertation defense. In some fields, one may be required to orally defend a dissertation, but also respond to questions purposely chosen from other, predetermined fields of study to ensure the graduate has achieved sufficient breadth of knowledge in related fields. In other fields, the questioning is restricted to the content of the dissertation, the final presentation a true test, with "pass" or "fail" grades hanging in the balance. Successful outcome is a foregone conclusion in other instances; the defense a formality with merely ceremonial significance.

The North American dissertation defense may require suit-and-tie formality; the procedure, or, more accurately, the ceremony, is very different in Europe. A senior Canadian professor was invited to spend a semester as a visiting professor in Holland; toward the end of his visit, he was invited to be a member of a dissertation committee as an external examiner. On the fateful day, the panelists and audience, all decked out in formal academic hoods, convened in a beautiful medieval hall. The young candidate, also formally garbed, strode in and took his place. The ceremony began with an announcer banging a heavy staff on the old stone floor. There was respectful silence in the hall. Each member of the examining panel asked a question in turn, and the student responded. The language used was, of course, Dutch. The Canadian professor, a visitor and honorary panelist, was last to ask a question. Not very knowledgeable in the particular field of study, and unable to follow the language well, he opted to ask a more philosophical question. The poor student was stumped, and began to stammer a response. Due to the language barrier, the visitor was unaware that all previous questions were very simple, and the student had been made aware in advance of the questions for the ceremony. The dissertation "defense" was, in fact, a symbolic and colorful celebratory forum. The flustered youngster continued to struggle for an answer to this unexpected question; the announcer suddenly returned, again banged his staff on the stone floor. Precisely one hour had passed, and the red-faced student had been saved by the "bell."

Most PhD programs in the United States take four to five years, at least on paper; the average time to completion is longer, and some students spend as many as ten years or more on their PhD. In recent years, some programs have been encouraging students to graduate sooner, while other programs (the life and biological sciences) have been going in the opposite direction, allowing more time for completion. Some arguments in favor state that extensions allow students more time for marriage, children, and other important achievements in life. Students are also able to publish more before their tenure clock starts ticking. Critics of extensions argue that they are implemented to allow principal investigators better access to cheap labor in their laboratories, or that they encourage students to procrastinate.

Registering the Approved Dissertation

As the adrenalin high of passing the dissertation defense subsides, one potentially maddening task remains; submitting the final and approved written dissertation document to the relevant school of graduate studies within the university. This may seem trivial, but frequently is not; the submitted document must conform precisely to a very strict set of requirements. These guidelines include: filling out various forms and ensuring they are signed properly by the advisor and committee members; utilizing acceptable paper types, text styles, typefaces and sizes, as well as text spacing; incorporating figures and charts using approved colors and styles; numbering pages using the appropriate norms; and the ever-maddening margin rules. The margins are important because the submitted manuscript is often destined to be bound and displayed in the university's collection.

The student is typically required to set an appointment for this final submission, during which a university representative will painstakingly review each and every submitted document, beginning with confirmation of all required signatures. This person, in the student's agonized presence, frequently pulls out a ruler and carefully measures the margins around the text. She ensures all the pages are sequentially numbered, and generally picks on every tiny detail, all of which leads the student to conclude that the school really is trying to drive him mad. Woe to a student whose margins are off by an eighth of an inch! He'll have to reprint the entire paper, set a new appointment with the bureaucrat, at which time the maddening process will be repeated—the last thing any sleep-deprived student wants to do! The delay can be especially upsetting when it may make the student ineligible for the upcoming graduation ceremonies—the student may be forced to wait as long as a year before formally graduating.

One amusing dissertation submission story dates back to the 1970s (student's name withheld to protect his identity). The now-ubiquitous word processor wasn't yet a glimmer in Seymour Rubenstein's or Rob Barnaby's eyes; all dissertations had to be typed on a good old-fashioned machine known, quaintly, as a typewriter. The submitted copy had to be flawless, so many students spent a lot of time typing and retyping, an unthinkable process these days. This particular student believed he finally had the necessary letter-perfect dissertation manuscript and set up an appointment for submission. The night before, he flipped lazily through the large manuscript and realized, to his horror, that he'd skipped a page number at the beginning of the dissertation! There was no physical way he could retype the entire document overnight, and he would undoubtedly have lost his mind in the process anyway. Determined to get through the next day's formality (and perhaps applying the initiative he'd learned as a graduate student), he typed up a very neat-looking page containing complete gibberish, bearing the missing page number, and slipped it into the gap in the manuscript. The next day the university employee went through all the motions: he checked the margins, ensured the paper was of appropriate quality, and flipped quickly through the entire document, reading off the sequential page numbers. The ploy worked! Several weeks later the student entered the school library, found his now-professionally bound dissertation among the book stacks, flipped to the rogue page, and neatly (perhaps triumphantly) tore it out!

To avoid some of this agony, students can do themselves a big favor by getting the submission requirements well ahead of time, and, if at all possible, converting the dissertation to the required format as early as possible. It's also advisable to get signatures from committee members immediately after successfully defending the dissertation, as it can subsequently take many months to track them all down.

There is an upside to properly registering a dissertation. Usually, a copy is converted to digital form and incorporated into a large electronic library. Interested readers may then access the database of dissertations, read various portions, and request printed copies. In recent years, authors have become eligible for royalty payments whenever a copy of their dissertation is requested. Most dissertations attract a relatively small readership, however, so the cumulative royalties, however emotionally satisfying, are trivially small.

Chapter 4: Financing Graduate Education

The costs of a PhD vary greatly, and depend upon the institution (tuition, books, medical care, lab and student-body fees), the costs of living within commuting distance of the school (housing and transportation costs), and the time necessary to complete the coursework, research, dissertation, and employment search. Total annual expenses may be as high as $50,000 at the most prestigious private institutions. The full cost of a PhD in a public university may be as high as $20,000-$30,000 per year, where the bulk of the cost comes from living expenses, coupled with lower tuition fees.

In the best cases, a school will provide full support, also known as a "free ride," by waiving tuition, which in itself may amount to $30,000 or more, and will, in addition, provide a stipend or scholarship which may be in the range of $15,000–$20,000 annually. In most cases, this generous level of support will be limited to four years, following which the support may decline precipitously or entirely disappear. This decline is partly to avoid impoverishing the school providing the support, but is also meant to "encourage" the student to graduate.

Few people can shoulder the interest payment burden after borrowing $50,000 annually over the course of five or six years, so it's highly advisable to seek some source of income over this period. Surprisingly, or perhaps a testament to people's passion for an academic education, it's not unusual to encounter graduates who are managing over $150,000 in student loans. In some cases, part of this total is due to *undergraduate* debt.

There are, however, situations in which incoming students, often mature students with means, will request entrance to a PhD program, and offer to fully pay their own way. This allows the institution to admit the additional student without cutting back on entry spots or support for others, which can be a win-win for all concerned—as long as the incoming student is able to meet the academic entrance requirements.

Most PhD students receive a "package," consisting of some tuition relief and a stipend, and may also seek additional income as teaching or research assistants. In some cases, one's stipend is conditional on performing such functions. In addition, graduate students are often eligible for grants and loans from a variety of governments, not-for-profit organizations, and for-profit corporations. All prospective students should investigate the programs for which they are eligible. Military service veterans and members of minority groups may find additional programs designed specifically for their situation, and should take advantage of these wherever and whenever possible.

Supply and demand (university budgets, scholarship funds available and the number of students who require financial aid) determines a student's package: as noted above, some are "free rides" with scholarships and tuition waivers; others include one but not the other. Overstretched and overenrolled programs may even force incoming students to compete for small numbers of scholarships, with the less-fortunate students having to pay full tuition or drop out. This may occur at even the wealthiest schools. In some cases, examination results determine which students retain or receive financial support.

Financial support differs significantly from department to department and from Faculty to Faculty. The "laboratory sciences" (biology, chemistry, medicine, physics, engineering) rely heavily on grants from governments and other institutions. The more prestigious an academic institution, the more grant money it can attract, and the better conditions it can offer to its students. An institution's reputation plays a significant role throughout the educational experience and beyond graduation to securing employment. Ironically, and perhaps counter-intuitively for some, an institution's good reputation can actually lead to worse financial conditions for students. Some institutions are so highly regarded that they can get away with offering students very little. The program's reputation draws many applicants willing to go into debt in exchange for a degree with a brand name.

Students the world over are expected to suffer as part of their apprenticeship—and many do. Thousands struggle to get by on $10,000 to $15,000 a year. During these lean years, dining out, vacations, birthday presents, electronic gadgets, and all manner of non-essential expenditures are beyond reach. In some cases, nutrition suffers, leading to ill health.

Given the length and intensity of a PhD program, the reality of financial hardships cannot be ignored. Nevertheless, the most solid advice still seems to be "Get into the best program you can. Don't base your decision on financial considerations in the short term." The logic is that it's better to suffer economically for four to five years, and reap the fruits of a good education with a very good job, rather than have it easier in those initial years, and find it much more difficult to get a decent job for the rest of one's career. It's easy to give such advice and forget that a student may have obligations such as family, making financial support very important in the decision-making process. Ultimately, each student must make her own decision based on personal circumstances and preferences. Nevertheless, in general, one should strive to get into the best program possible.

It's never too early to begin the search for funding! Lengthy delays between initial applications and receipt of funds are common, so it's wise to apply early. Missed deadlines can mean waiting a whole year before the window of opportunity reopens. Make the most compelling case possible to maximize the likelihood of gaining much-needed funds; it's important to be very precise and follow all instructions. Thousands of applications are rejected every year simply because students fail to complete them properly: lending institutions tend to suppose that a person who can't or won't follow simple instructions to get money isn't going to be reliable in repaying it.

The search for funding is highly competitive; all applicants do their best to distinguish themselves, presenting themselves as likely to succeed in their education, making the investment in their future work seem sensible. There is no point in hastily sending out fifty grant applications if each of them is sloppy. The odds of success are much better with ten carefully, conscientiously prepared applications.

Some combination of the following sources of funding will likely be available:

- Grants
- Fellowships
- Loans
- Teaching assistantships
- Research assistantships
- Summer internships
- Provincial and state support
- Merit scholarships
- Minority grants
- University grants
- Support from charitable foundations, government agencies, and military benefits

In North America, some of the more common sources of funding are grants from the American National Science Foundation (NSF), Canadian National Science and Engineering Research Council (NSERC) and Social Sciences and Humanities Research Council of Canada (SSHRC).

There are many books and manuals available for students to pursue each of these options. Each university will have information regarding additional sources of funding. Occasionally, special grants are available to minority groups or for research in particular fields. Foreign students usually have a harder time qualifying for many grants, fellowships, and loans.

Some More Innovative Funding Options

Inclusion of these examples does not constitute endorsement!

- One student reportedly showed up at school one morning with a myriad of multicolored tubes sticking out of his nose and wrapped around his head and body, culminating in an equally colorful set of plastic containers fastened about him. To make ends meet, he'd decided to forego the usual options and responded to an advertisement in the nearby research hospital. The advertisement called for male subjects in a particular age range for a four-week experiment. This required him to sleep in the hospital over that period, and be subjected to various highly invasive tests.

- Another student, in Japan, reportedly responded to an advertisement by a condom-manufacturing firm. He was required to create a mold using a certain part of his anatomy.

- Occasionally, there are advertisements in student newspapers, seeking egg donors. These usually list a very specific profile requirement for the donor—age range, height and weight, educational and social background, sometimes ethnic origin.

- It's not unusual to come across a story of a graduate student financing studies by moonlighting as an exotic dancer.

Given the ongoing debate regarding the morality of some of these activities, a student is well-advised to consider all the repercussions and implications.

Chapter 5: Surviving the PhD Program

Mathematician: a machine for turning coffee into theorems. - Anonymous

A PhD program isn't a project to be entered into on a whim or as an afterthought. Some students describe how they got into law school, business school, or medical school with "I wrote the LSAT/GMAT/MCAT, and I did okay, so I thought, what the hell, I'll apply to a few schools, and I got in." This may seem cool or fortuitous, but is a recipe for disaster if it's the attitude leading to enrollment in a PhD program. Getting a PhD is a formidable undertaking which involves a very rigorous and emotionally draining course of study, completion of several years of high-level coursework, comprehensive examinations, defense of a dissertation proposal, and final defense of a completed dissertation. Each phase is challenging, calls for different skills, and is designed to ensure that a student masters both basic and advanced material in a highly specialized field.

This chapter addresses the skills and discipline necessary to survive the ordeal, the significant difficulties in completing the program, and the implications of leaving empty-handed.

What It Takes to Complete a Doctoral Program

The complex demands of a doctoral program call for a diverse set of traits and skills. While no student exhibits mastery of all the needed attributes, the more she has, the better her chances of prevailing.

A student should possess, or plan to acquire early in the program, as many of the following skills as possible:

- Organization. The organized student keeps a comprehensive calendar, plans ahead, sets realistic timelines, develops an efficient filing system for articles, working papers, and conference proceedings, maintains thorough course and research notes, uses time wisely, orders critical materials well in advance of deadlines, and has the discipline to maintain these habits over prolonged periods. Being organized means being productive—making every week count—steadily making tangible progress, leading to greater predictability of output, and benefiting from a consistent feeling that her time is used positively and constructively. Disorganized students waste a lot of time and resources, delaying progress.

- Maturity. The mature student has a high measure of personal integrity, puts setbacks into perspective and overcomes them, is honestly introspective, assessing her performance realistically, learns from her mistakes and avoids repeating them. She identifies symptoms of stress, frustration, burnout and depression accurately, and understands herself well enough to know how to deal with reversals, including soothing her own anxiety through a hobby or some other constructive outlet. The frustrations associated with any doctoral program make it inevitable that students will need to draw on their maturity and poise.

- Self motivation. The motivated student is able to sustain her passion for the subject, fueling an inner source of renewable energy. She is able to maintain a solid pace and commitment during the inevitable downtimes, when lowered morale can lead to disorientation and procrastination. Self-motivation is particularly necessary during the less-structured dissertation phase to sustain the momentum toward subject mastery and new discovery.

- Focus. The focused student exhibits commitment and tenacity, pursues objectives patiently, consciously chooses constructive steps and makes necessary personal sacrifices to meet objectives. She is not easily distracted, doesn't procrastinate or indulge in useless tangents.

- Flexibility and adaptability. The flexible student approaches challenges, both personal and professional, from different angles, believing she will find solutions, refusing to succumb to frustration. She analyzes negative feedback carefully, takes any constructive content positively and shrugs off the rest. A doctoral program has a number of phases, which require very different skills, in addition to unpredictable changes that require her to adapt and move on.

- Creativity. Qualifying for a PhD requires original work; the creative student progresses by critically evaluating the field's accepted knowledge, asking "why" and "how" questions to generate her own original thoughts and approaches. Creative students have the potential to produce truly original work and open up new fields; the ability to meld creativity with disciplined scholarship marks the leaders.

- Intelligence. Graduate students must be intelligent to qualify for the program: each has the raw brain power to assess methodologies, theories, plans and results, and recognize unfounded assumptions that yield flawed results.

- Skepticism. A skeptical student recognizes that human beings make errors; she thinks and questions carefully and accepts ideas as working theories, subject to proofs, because academe abounds with preconceived notions, flawed assumptions, and incorrect conclusions.

- Emotional competence. An emotionally aware student connects emotionally with others by exhibiting empathy and understanding. She masters her emotions and communicates effectively with others, be they professors, peers, or pupils. She treats people equally and respectfully, regardless of their station in life.

- Courage. Standing up before an audience of experts and exposing one's precious work to criticism requires courage, especially if her conclusions clash with mainstream views or suggest controversial alternative hypotheses. The courageous student makes important decisions, acts boldly when necessary, stands up for her principles in the classroom, and continues her work in the face of her own, and others', doubts.

- Open-mindedness. The open-minded student sees merit in questioning "sacred cows" and listening fully to the ideas of others. She recognizes that her ideas aren't necessarily superior to those of others, and differentiates between leaps of intuition and jumping to conclusions.

- Writing skills. "Publish or Perish!" is the essence of the academic experience. Writing succinctly, clearly and persuasively to convey thoughts, ideas, and research results with others is the foundation of scholarly pursuits. Brilliant research presented in dull, dry tomes goes unnoticed, unappreciated, and denies important discoveries and answers to others seeking knowledge. Learning to write well requires effort, time and focus, and should be considered a prerequisite to any postgraduate program.

- Reading skills. Reading quickly while retaining important content is a primary skill at every academic level, beginning in kindergarten. Communication among academics is primarily through the written word: reading and comprehending the thoughts and results documented by others is critical to subject mastery and original contributions.

- Presentation skills. Sharing thoughts and ideas effectively with others is necessary to developing one's career. If an audience has difficulty understanding a presenter, their first inclination is to discount the presenter's data or her credibility, or both. Confident, articulate presenters who draw their listeners into their subject are most likely to be in demand in conference and lecture settings: after all the hard study, research, laboratory tedium and drafting, writing and polishing papers, a student owes it to herself to deliver a refined presentation to appreciative audiences.

Risk Awareness and Management

Members of the academic community (professors and graduate students) face a myriad of risks, some specific to academia, others inherent in living. Fortunately, while there are many risks, most are relatively trivial in the sense that the damage or loss they may lead to is fairly small.

An example of risk specific to academe is the probability that one's area of research has been explored and reported by someone else. The severity of outcome may range from minor embarrassment to a law suits for plagiarism or patent infringement.

Risks can be classified into categories, including, among others, financial risks, health or physical risks, operational and reputation risks. The example dealing with unoriginal research may be classified as a reputation risk. Members of the academic community face risks in all these categories.

Some of the specific risks academics face:

- Selecting an advisor without being certain of his commitment to his students
- Including unknown people on one's dissertation committee
- Electing not to study more for a course or exam
- Juggling too many projects
- Running an experiment without process controls or documentation
- Choosing not to protect artwork against water damage or temperature changes, or

- Forgetting to back up electronic files, including one's dissertation

It's not possible to be fully prepared for every risk, but it's reckless not to mitigate easily identifiable risks. Each of the risks listed above can be mitigated to some extent. It is nothing short of irresponsible to fail to act prudently to reduce risks. Getting to know faculty members, speaking to their students, backing up all computer files, buying appropriate insurance, documenting all laboratory processes, keeping sensitive materials and products in a safe place, along with all other reasonable contingency plans, is simple common sense and a function of maturity.

A wise student recognizes risks, respects them, and acknowledges that risk-taking is a fact of life, both personally and professionally. He also understands the logic of working to reduce risks wherever possible, and to proactively manage remaining risks, particularly when long hours of studying and research can dull one's senses and responses.

The Most Difficult Thing about Being a PhD Student

An often-repeated joke is that the most difficult thing about the PhD program is getting one's entire dissertation committee in one room, at one time, for the final defense. This particular effort can indeed be very frustrating, but there are, unfortunately, many other aspects of a PhD program which prove to be very difficult and, for some people, these obstacles prove insurmountable.

Doctoral programs are lengthy and complex; the students enrolled in them are so different, there is no single challenge that clearly dominates all others. Here is some feedback compiled from PhD graduates in response to the question: "What was the most difficult part of your PhD program?"

Many identified the *comprehensive examinations* as the most difficult: the reference wasn't to the testing day itself, but rather the agonizing, stress-filled months of preparations for the actual test that appear to suck the life out of people—significant deterioration in the physical appearance and demeanor in those preparing for the dreaded day is fairly common. The relevant body of material covered by these examinations is immense, regardless of the program. Many students begin studying, and, several months before the exam suddenly realize that, at their current pace, they simply won't be able to cover all the required material. This realization forces them to spend longer hours studying, allowing themselves fewer opportunities to recharge batteries, creating ever-increasing pressure.

Others found the *coursework* most challenging: PhD programs often call for several years of in-class course work, often taught by gung-ho (young and/or highly motivated) professors eager to exercise rigor (an admirable approach). Their highly challenging curricula may call for very dense reading lists, covering dozens of books and/or journal articles. Struggling to handle the course work, students have too little time to make progress on research and dissertation topics. Worse still, much required course content doesn't qualify as easy bedtime reading, regardless of the passion a student has for the subject. Frankly, items on such reading lists are often of interest to very few people in the world, one of whom is typically the professor teaching the course.

Others suggested the *dissertation* phase as most difficult: the dissertation phase can be so frustrating a surprising proportion of students—in good standing— find they can't bear the strain, and leave the program. Sometimes, departure is the consequence of the student's emotional or intellectual immaturity; younger students are challenged by graduate-level coursework, but are still in their element within the natural structure of assignment due dates, known curricula, and set examination dates. Once the dissertation phase begins, most or all that structure disappears: those who cannot or do not have the initiative, drive, and focus are frequently beset by confusion, frustration, and self-doubt.

Making a *presentation* to local faculty members or another academic audience is the graduate-school version of the dread of public speaking. The stress may come from concern about appearing ignorant of the literature, having misunderstood the true significance of the literature, making simple and unforgivable mistakes in modeling or analysis, being unable to respond to the simplest questions, speaking so feebly everyone in the room will think them weak and pathetic, or getting emotional and bursting into tears. The dread can lead the student to believe he's the stupidest person in the world, destined to make a fool of himself, and forever lose the respect of his professors.

An added source of anxiety during presentations—informal or formal—is the presence of one or more professors intent on undermining students: these critics are frequently trying to prove that they are smarter than everyone else in the room, including the hapless student-speaker being subjected to the barbed comments. Knowing that the same professors treat every student presenter the same way is not particularly comforting, but other, more mature professors usually discount the heckler's comments and feedback.

Some other responses to the question included: "Just the first five years," and "I have no complaints other than my advisor having PMS every day for five years!" (For the record, her advisor was a man.)

One of the simplest, but most powerful, responses: "The *fear* that I wasn't good enough" (the same as the fear of being identified as "an admissions committee mistake"). This concern gnaws away at some students from the moment they are notified of acceptance to a program, and may rear its ugly head whenever there is even a minor setback on the long path to the PhD. The associated anxiety may accumulate to become debilitating, as it strips away a student's confidence and renders him resigned to failure.

Finally, another very difficult aspect of the PhD program is the *decision to walk away*. Students tend not to talk too much about this because it opens a very personal window into humiliation and embarrassment. Leaving the PhD program is a very dramatic outcome and deserves additional attention.

Leaving Without the PhD

Attrition rates within PhD programs vary by program and institution. It's not unusual for these to range between 30 and 50 percent. Typically, the largest proportion of dropouts make their decision to leave by the time comprehensive examinations are written, which usually occurs a year or two into the program. The second largest attrition occurs during the dissertation phase.

In some cases (for example, in the United States), students may qualify for a master's degree when departing just before or after comprehensive examinations. Such degrees are often thought of as consolation prizes.

There are only two ways to leave a PhD program: involuntarily and voluntarily.

Leaving Involuntarily

Schools initiate the separation if the student has formally failed an important phase of the program, or when it appears that failure is inevitable.

Most students realize well in advance that dismissal is coming; nonetheless, it is a very painful and embarrassing message to hear. It's natural to feel embarrassed, humiliated, hurt, resentful, offended, and even betrayed, but it's important to put the experience in perspective.

Should these people label themselves as failures? Do others have the right to label them as failures? Should this be allowed to affect a student's sense of personal worth? Should he be devastated?

The answer to all the above is, emphatically, No!

The individuals in question managed to get into the program because they had already excelled academically, and likely performed well on other prerequisites such as standardized tests. The very admission to the program confirms a series of achievements and reflects separation from a large crowd of hopefuls. To put things in perspective, according to the U.S. Census Bureau *Current Population Survey 2004*, about 16 percent of the population over the age of 15 hold one university degree. Roughly 7 percent hold a master's degree, and only 1 percent hold a PhD degree. In other words, the mere acceptance into a doctoral program is already an unusual achievement. The end of one's PhD aspirations may seem, at the time, a huge disaster: however, in academic achievement they still rank in the top 15 percent, perhaps top 7 percent, of the population—a significant accomplishment.

It's easy and predictable for some of the affected people to ignore logic, wallow in personal misery, and seriously doubt their own intellect and calling in life. Before succumbing to labeling people as stupid or inadequate, it's important to ask questions: Is it possible that the person did not succeed because, deep down, he simply didn't have the commitment? Or that, deep down, he really wasn't cut out for theoretical research?

Most people fail PhD programs simply because the program isn't sufficiently compelling and thrilling: we all know highly intelligent people who require great intellectual stimulation. There is no shame in leaving because the program isn't satisfactory. In fact, this book is written to help people recognize, in advance, whether they have the appropriate level of interest and commitment for a PhD program.

Countless people who don't complete their PhD program go on to become outstanding successes in business and industry. Once outside the ivory tower, they begin to realize just how insulated they had been from the rest of the world. There are infinite possibilities in the "real world," and many avenues to fulfilling lives and careers. Rather than being humiliated, students should recognize that learning sooner rather than later their bliss is not a PhD gives them more time to seek a fulfilling career elsewhere.

Leaving Voluntarily

Students initiate the departure for any of a myriad of reasons: a change in personal interests, reluctance to maintain the student lifestyle, a change in family situation, financial constraints, transfer to another program, or transfer to another university. Again, a main reason for writing this book is to emphasize that too many people don't fully understand the reality of intense academic pursuits; it's not much of a surprise if they do decide to move on to other pursuits.

Fear of being stigmatized and labeled a failure makes the decision to leave voluntarily difficult: the longer the student has been at the school, the more difficult the choice. Those who are able to take a close look at themselves and their personal needs and aspirations, and set aside stigma and embarrassment, are to be commended for making a respectable decision.

Persevering in a doctoral program despite a lack of interest in an academic career can lead to perverse outcomes down the road. Hiring committees and corporate human resources personnel have been known to reject candidates with PhDs due to concerns they may be over-qualified for non-academic positions.

All the points made in the "Involuntary" section of this text apply here as well. The decision to leave should represent a move to bigger and better things, not a reason to be embarrassed or indulge in self-doubt. Those who choose to leave voluntarily are ahead of the game with respect to those who are told to leave, because they have already concluded their future is elsewhere, and have the courage to go find it.

The Mental Health of the PhD Student

The strains and stresses associated with doctoral programs can be very significant, and have been known to shatter confidence, cause very serious depression and feelings of inadequacy. Sadly, instead of producing powerful, confident scholars, our existing academic systems often produce shy, withdrawn, timid, and self-conscious graduates.

Some of the factors that negatively affect graduate students include (in no particular order):

- Immense pressure to produce unique research
- Stress of high work load and very difficult examinations
- Loneliness
- Inevitable setbacks and disappointments
- Financial constraints
- Family problems
- Self–doubt, and
- Inability to see light at the end of the tunnel

The critical message here is to keep one's studies in perspective, and not allow these stresses to affect health. Setbacks are a time for review and assessment, but should not be taken too personally. *Success or failure in a doctoral program doesn't define a person or her personal worth.*

To deal with the inevitable setbacks, it's useful to have a safety net in place. This may include nurturing a confidant to share concerns, or finding a supporter among the faculty who can help more objectively gauge the severity and implications of a setback. If the stress becomes overwhelming, it may be appropriate to consider seeking professional help. Most schools have mental health facilities available, and a struggling student should take advantage of such resources. There is no shame in seeking help.

The Joys of Being a PhD Student

So far the discussion has emphasized the stresses, the hurdles, the heartaches, the setbacks, and the disappointments of a PhD program. To be sure, there are happy moments as well—completing a course or a paper, finishing an exam, relief at completing the dreaded first presentation (not always a fun experience, but makes the relief that much stronger), passing the comprehensive exams, and the excitement of that first meaningful scientific discovery. Depending on the program of study, discovery may come in the form of a mathematical derivation, a significant empirical measurement, or unearthing a special historical document. That new discovery or unique achievement is the joy and essence of academic research; a student who can't get excited by discovery *should be* rethinking his career choice.

So, yes, there are moments of joy and happiness during the program. All students (to varying degrees) are bolstered and encouraged the first time they do really well on an exam or project, or receive a satisfying grade. There is a definite sense of accomplishment at completing the formal requirements at the end of each semester's coursework, and at the end of each school year. There is an unmistakable sense of relief after writing that last exam, marking the end of coursework forever!

These much-needed positive moments may seem few and far between. Enhancing the number of positive experiences from non-academic sources—hobbies, extracurricular athletics or club activities, or just taking walks—and supporting themselves emotionally and physically enriches students' personal and academic experiences. Graduate school coincides with beginning a family for many students; welcoming that first child can be a marvelous and uplifting experience that, while exhausting, can be inspirational and provides much-needed perspective. Suddenly a failed experiment doesn't seem as devastating when one is thankful for having a healthy family.

Then, of course, there is the ultimate highlight: that moment when all the work is completed. It's quite difficult to put that emotion into words—a combination of relief, exhaustion, and adrenaline, the memorable sense of a weight being lifted off one's shoulders, followed by a distinct, surprising serenity and relaxed satisfaction. Many are moved to tears when they finally have an opportunity to dwell on the immensity of their achievement. Tears and relief are often the first recognition of just how stressful the process has been.

Many students are so emotionally exhausted by graduation time, so worried about job placements and tenure clocks they forget to reward themselves for all their hard work. Enjoy the thrill of completing the program, of navigating the furthest reaches of human intellectual pursuits. Separate yourself from the fast track for a few days, savor the accomplishment! There will be plenty of time for all the other tasks later.

Chapter 6: The Postdoctoral Fellowship

Submitting the approved dissertation was described as the last battle of the PhD program in an earlier chapter. While this is technically the case, it's hardly the last hurdle for the aspiring academic to overcome.

A professorship in any academic field requires the demonstrated ability to undertake meaningful research, evident in articles printed in peer reviewed journals, especially in leading publications. Some fields allow new PhDs to secure tenure-track assistant professorships with just their unpublished thesis. Most fields, however, require a selection of peer reviewed publications for consideration for tenure-track positions: the more competitive the field, the more publications in leading journals may be required.

Given these requirements, an intermediate step exists between completion of the PhD and qualification for a tenure-track job in some fields; a postdoctoral fellowship (postdoc) may last one or two years and may be arranged within a variety of academic institutions (universities, research laboratories, or think tanks).

The postdoc can be thought of as a finishing school for graduate students; an opportunity to continue research efforts, amass additional publications, hone teaching and presentation skills, learn new techniques, be exposed to new ways of looking at the world, and develop a wider network of personal relationships with others in the field. Nurturing these contacts may be very important for a person's development and broadening of her horizons. It can also be a useful period for those who aren't exactly sure what they want to do long-term or whose dissertation and/or publication records are not quite compelling enough to obtain a good position. Some refer to the postdoc as the minor leagues of research, but this can be an unfair characterization. "Minor league" implies a lesser talent; there is no reason for a postdoctoral fellow's work to be inferior. Many of the world's leading scientists paid their dues as postdoctoral fellows. It is, perhaps, better thought of as a rite of passage.

Students who accept fellowships in the same institution that granted them a PhD don't get the benefit of a new environment and diverse experiences; one should avoid remaining in the same university for both PhD and postdoc. Sometimes, however, following the doctoral dissertation, an advisor won't release the student because she wants him to finish various projects, and may have him installed as a postdoc. This is in the professor's best interest, but not always in the student's best interest.

The search for a postdoc position begins about six months prior to the end of one's PhD. The search should be undertaken with the help of one's advisor, who is expected to use her contacts to find an ideal placement for the student. Some professors are more helpful than others during this process. As discussed in an earlier section, evaluating a prospective advisor's willingness to help in this function before signing on to work with her is wise.

The competition to join some academic departments is so fierce, only postdocs need apply. A "mere" PhD graduate does not yet have a sufficient publication record to even merit attention. As a prerequisite for applying to permanent positions, some institutions now require as many as three postdocs—over six years! This level of competition is associated with the best departments in the world. There may be less competition in a large number of state and land-grant universities and teachers colleges; some require only one postdoc, and others may place greater emphasis on teaching rather than research accomplishments, and do not require any postdoctoral work.

The postdoc experience can be quite difficult. Postdocs receive a salary or stipend, but it's usually not much more than a graduate student's pittance. While one has the benefit of being referred to as

"Doctor," there are virtually no financial benefits. Postdocs may become dissertation advisors for PhD students; some postdocs can be PIs (heads of laboratories). Despite being eligible for such responsible roles, postdocs are viewed in some circumstances as highly sophisticated, yet cheap, labor. A postdoc may be held back by an unscrupulous PI or advisor who wishes to capitalize on her ability to generate publications (enhancing the laboratory's prestige), write grant applications (improving the laboratory's financial situation), and help to mentor others (saving the PI time and effort); these are extreme situations, however, and avoidable by choosing advisors and PIs carefully.

A soon-to-be PhD graduate is well advised to decide early on whether she is interested in pressing on with an academic career or an external industry position. Postdocs typically receive a salary, but it's always quite modest: deciding not to pursue the postdoc and spend one's time more productively on an industry job search can be far more rewarding and less frustrating.

Some postdocs stay on as postdocs for years, unwilling to move on; a few, known as professional postdocs, remain postdocs forever. Unable to make it to the next level as professors, many end up as glorified technicians.

Following postdoc completion, the ideal outcome is to be offered a tenure-track position. Occasionally, the department where the postdoc is completed may want the student to stay on in an adjunct role, but will not offer a more permanent position. The reason is simple: the department already has the person in its clutches, so why waste a tenure-track professorship on him? If the candidate is good at raising money, he may be offered an adjunct position where his salary comes from money he raises—rather like commissions on sales. However, the university is much more likely to offer a tenure track, because a postdoc good at fund-raising is likely to be offered a tenure-track elsewhere, and take the funding with him.

Chapter 7: Finding Employment

Just when the PhD student is finally getting into a good rhythm with her dissertation work, she is distracted by the need to begin the job-search process. The uncompromising timelines of the job-search force students to expend significant time and energy exactly when that time is needed to complete the dissertation.

Setting aside the annoyance factor, the job search is very important and does require time and energy. One can ill afford to ignore the need to plan ahead and make a good impression on recruiters. Unfortunately, many students are so exhausted by the end of their dissertation that they have no energy left for a job search, damaging their employment prospects.

Depending on the field of study, a conditional job offer may be received before the PhD is completed, typically requiring the new employee be awarded the PhD within a year of taking on the position.

Some of the earliest challenges a student faces are in deciding which of the following three job markets to pursue:

- Academic
- Corporate
- Government

It is possible to pursue any combination of these in parallel, but each leads to a different career path and life choices. The key is to identify a path one can thrive in, both emotionally and professionally. One important aspect of the decision is how you want to be viewed within society. According to a Harris poll conducted in 2006, scientists are among the most admired professionals in American society; business executives, stockbrokers and real estate agents are least admired. When you're deciding which path to take, it's best to first consider these questions carefully:

- Is it immensely important to you to be a member of the academic or scientific community?
- Would you feel you'd sold out your academic integrity by taking a job with a for-profit corporation?
- Do you feel a calling to public service in a government agency, or do you view such environments as mediocre and bureaucratic?
- Is your objective to maximize earnings potential?

Assessing the importance of financial considerations in your decision-making process is a first step.

Compensation

The overall state of pay for people in the academic community with PhDs has long been the subject of jokes—uniformly dark humor. In reality, the pain isn't shared equally across programs of study; some graduates are able to command much higher academic starting salaries in fields that lend themselves to commercial applications, primarily because universities must compete with industry salaries to have any chance at hiring and retaining faculty members.

Some fields most affected by external opportunities and salary inflation are finance, biotech, engineering, and law. Graduates of finance programs benefit from the demand for such skills on Wall

Street. Those with degrees in the biological sciences are often wooed by pharmaceutical companies. Engineering firms and high-tech start-ups may be lucrative alternatives for graduates of science and engineering programs. Law graduates can often find high-paying positions in private practice.

A graduate with a PhD in humanities or social sciences may expect to be offered much less compensation than a graduate from some of the fields listed above. Actual numbers in 2009 could easily be $140,000 for a graduate from a finance PhD program, compared to a salary of $40,000-$50,000 for a graduate with an English Literature PhD.

These differences are quite staggering, and seem unfair to those with lesser compensation potential. Nevertheless, this is reality.

Choosing to pursue a PhD degree is a significant step in shaping one's career. A student owes it to herself to be aware of the financial implications of her choice, including the realization that certain academic paths do not command high salaries. Many PhD degree holders end up employed in some activity only vaguely associated with, sometimes entirely unrelated to, their field of study. Most PhD applicants know ahead of time that, upon graduation, they may have to take their hard-earned doctorates and stuff them in the attic if they intend to support themselves and/or a family.

The full financial implications of a chosen course of study must be taken into consideration, but the student's final decision should come down to her passion for the subject. Passion will sustain the individual during lean years; yearning for status and salary may sustain a person through a two-year graduate degree, but surviving a rigorous five-year PhD requires deeper commitment than just future salary expectations.

Salary is also heavily affected by the wealth and prestige of the degree-granting institution. For the most part, wealthy institutions pay more. Interestingly, however, there are cases where a very prestigious institution will not be the highest-paying. The argument in these cases is that the employee gains a real benefit from the institution's prestige, allowing the institution to get away with paying less.

Preparation for the Job Search

The tenured job search is a critical phase in an academic's life. Ideally, a person is able to find a position where he is happy to put down roots permanently, enjoy the stimulating intellectual environment of the institution, and grow professionally alongside his peers and friends.

Needless to say, few employment opportunities provide such an idyllic outcome, and those that do are fiercely contested by eligible candidates. Each job seeker must make the best impression possible; recruiters look for high-quality research and good teaching skills. The challenge for all job seekers is to market themselves effectively, successfully convincing their target audience of potential employers that they truly have these capabilities and skills.

Preparation must begin well in advance of graduation; in North America, the academic year extends from July to June. New professors typically come on board in July, allowing them roughly two months to settle in before teaching duties begin. As early as September of the previous year—almost a year before graduation—a student must begin preparations for recruiting events by:

- Creating a detailed *Curriculum Vitae*
- Soliciting reference letters from faculty members
- Putting the finishing touches on a job market paper and abstract
- Polishing presentation and interviewing skills

Advisors dedicated to their students' success will participate actively.

Curriculum Vitae

Curriculum Vitae (*CV*) is a Latin expression, literally, "course of life." *CV* is often used interchangeably with the French word, *résumé*. *CV* is the more correct format for academic settings; the less-rigid structure of a résumé is more often used in the private sector. Both documents list a person's accomplishments, including both educational background and work experience, and are used to apply for jobs.

A person's *CV* should be comprehensive, properly emphasizing noteworthy achievements. Given the importance of a *CV* for catching the attention of recruiters, edit and re-edit the *CV* until it clearly and neatly represents your accomplishments and potential. Ideally, a *CV* should be individually tailored to each employment opportunity, because different emphasis may be required, depending on the market being pursued. *CVs* for academic career applications must contain an expansive description of the candidate's publication record and teaching experience, and may easily be 4-12 pages long. An established professor's *CV* may be 50 pages long! Résumés for corporate positions should begin with work experiences and emphasize how PhD studies and other experiences have prepared the applicant for corporate employment: a résumé should be 1 or 2 pages; the average corporate recruiter won't have the time or inclination to read through a longer document.

Reference Letters

Reference letters are written by credible people willing to recommend the student for a particular position; a student's dissertation advisor and members of her dissertation committee generally write reference letters. Three reference letters, geared to the targeted market, are usually required. Some reference providers write a more general letter, but all reference letters should emphasize the research and teaching prowess of a candidate seeking an academic appointment.

References from academics are less common when corporate positions are sought. If these are required, however, remember that some professors may not view a student's decision to pursue a corporate career favorably; it may be sensible to approach non-academics when requesting recommendation letters for non-academic positions. Alternatively, if a student can show she's made an honest effort at academic positions without success, professors may be amenable to helping her seek non-academic employment.

Many professors are reluctant to put their own credibility on the line by providing a ringing endorsement of a mediocre candidate, especially if the candidate intends to send the letters to recruiters at the most prestigious institutions. An open and honest discussion between the student and the professor is necessary. Professors will sometimes give the student a choice: writing a reasonably positive endorsement for applications directed at less-prestigious institutions, or a letter containing a more subdued recommendation directed at first-tier schools. Since a less-than-ringing endorsement will immediately raise eyebrows by recruiters, it's generally not advisable to apply to "name" schools with a less-than-glowing recommendation. The professor may give the student a choice of letters; but, as a practical matter, the less-accomplished student should realize and accept that he is being directed to focus on schools where he has a better opportunity. Of course, the student always has the choice of seeking someone else to write a stronger recommendation letter.

A professor may refuse outright to write a reference letter, for legitimate reasons. One, the professor doesn't believe she knows the student's work well enough; two, she does know the student and has a low opinion of his abilities; three, she simply doesn't have the time to do an adequate job of writing such an important letter. Rather than dwelling on the reasons and feeling sorry for himself, the student should seek a reference from someone else.

Despite all this logic, some students coerce reluctant professors into writing letters, leading to a Pyrrhic victory. The reference letter they obtain is so watered down and lacking commitment that it serves as a warning to prospective employers, who quickly turn the candidate down.

Job Market Paper

The job market paper is the one document that aims to show employers the job seeker is capable of high-quality research. It is included with the *CV* or résumé. Ideally, the job market paper is a published article in one of the field's leading journals, providing immediate and incontrovertible proof that the author is highly capable of contributing to the literature at the highest level.

If the job market paper has not yet received the stamp of approval of a peer reviewed publication, it should still reflect a meaningful contribution to the literature, emphasizing the author's creativity and originality, grasp of important concepts in the field, and mastery of technical skills (such as statistical analysis). The quality and clarity of such papers is the strongest demonstration of a student's talent to prospective employers. Some students may have more than one article prepared, and may choose to emphasize one or the other, depending on the audience.

In some cases, the job market paper is a compilation of articles or papers, demonstrating the applicant's broad set of skills and contributions.

The professional appearance of the job market paper is crucial to a good impression. It must be well written, properly edited for accuracy, grammar, and format, and must provide real insight, displaying the author's talents and giving a glimpse of his potential as a contributor to the field of study.

Employers must be convinced of the applicant's talents. These are easiest to establish when the candidate is the only author of the job market paper. Joint research (a paper with multiple authors) always leaves the possibility that the applicant has relied heavily on another author's input. For jointly authored research, the advisor's reference letter can and should emphasize the candidate's primary contribution.

The candidate must also prepare a well-written abstract for all papers used in the process, because very few selection committee members have the time to read each and every full article submitted, and will most often focus on the much shorter abstracts to filter the many submissions. This means that for each paper, the abstract must provide insight into the applicant's creativity, technical skills, and writing ability.

Abstracts may also be submitted to journals and magazines, where they may be compiled and published. These publications may subsequently be viewed by a large number of researchers in a given field. Thus, the abstracts may serve as an advertisement of the applicant's skills to a large audience.

Presentation Skills

The ability to present well is critically important, regardless of whether one intends to pursue an academic, corporate, or government career.

A good presenter thinks carefully about the intended goals and audience for each of his presentations and practices accordingly. Slides, overheads, or graphics should emphasize the points to be made, but keep them clean and simple! If there is so much information the presenter is forced to read them mechanically, or the audience is straining to make out small print, the audience's interest is lost. Arguments should be built up logically; presenters should *not* assume any critical knowledge on the part of the audience. A natural reaction by a confused audience is to hold the presenter responsible; academics, particularly, don't think of themselves as stupid, so they generally hold it against a speaker when his session fails to make sense.

Learn to look at the audience and read individuals' reactions; adjust the tone and depth of the presentation in response. Some audiences want to dig into the tiniest details; others just want big-picture intuition. The presenter must be sensitive to these needs and amend the tone and complexity of his delivery; if the majority of attendees are lost, you've probably been too general; if the majority are bored, you've likely given too much detail.

Ask about the composition and sophistication level of the audience ahead of time and anticipate important questions. Such presentations are typically scheduled for 60 to 90 minutes, including time for questions and answers. Beginning and ending on time shows professionalism, although academicians are notorious for not adhering to clocks very well. Nevertheless, it's best to conclude as planned. The host or organizer of the recruiting event will likely signal when it's time to start and conclude; the best way to ensure time limits are respected is by rigorously practicing the presentation and anticipating typical questions.

Practice is the most important aspect of presentations: the presenter must come across as smooth, highly knowledgeable, and comfortable in the role of insight provider. The best ways to practice for job market presentations are by observing others presenting in similar forums and critiquing their performance, as well as taping one's own efforts and critiquing those. For job market preparation, it is useful to observe two types of speakers: very accomplished presenters who can set a high standard, and visiting students who are seeking to gain employment in your institution. Other students' experience will most likely reflect yours; note the types of questions the senior faculty members ask, and how the presenter reacts to these questions. A poised response is to be emulated.

As presentation settings differ, often based on a department's culture, a presenter may be treated delicately in one location, and relentlessly assailed in another. Try to determine the culture of the host institution well ahead of time to optimize preparation.

Practice by delivering a realistic presentation to a real audience; start with presenting to fellow students, even if you have to organize the forum. Keep in mind that it's far better to suffer some embarrassment in front of your peers than in front of a prospective employer. Videotaping is an excellent tool to identify technical and mechanical delivery issues—too much hand movement, speaking too quickly, or turning one's back to the audience. Once the student audience has given their constructive feedback, refine and present your talk again, this time to members of one's dissertation committee. Use the professors' feedback to improve your presentation further, and follow with a final session before the entire department, usually possible in an internal seminar series.

When responding to questions, think for a moment, ensure the question is properly understood, *then* answer succinctly, without getting pulled off on a tangent. Credible answers are very important; so is the confidence to say "I don't know." Resorting to "I don't know" too often isn't productive, but it's important to be honest and not pretend to have an answer—glibness is nearly always found out, and rarely forgiven. Making the effort to seek the answer and provide it at a later date to the person who brought it up comes across as professional.

Poise under cross-examination is critical, whether the inquiry comes from an academic seeking to test subject matter expertise, or a corporate recruiter focusing on practical intuition, it is important to exude confidence and stand up to pressure. Poise is prized in any setting.

It's not realistic to relay every detail of one's dissertation in a single hour; focus on the key points, logically laid out; if intuition is relevant, explain why you followed it, then discuss the implications of all you have presented. Details provided in response to specific questions are opportunities to convince the audience of the presenter's depth and breadth of knowledge.

A presenter isn't just putting forward academic subject matter; he is also presenting himself, and first impressions and physical appearance *does* matter. An ill-fitting suit, horrible tie, and dirty shoes are all bad ideas—a few *very* talented graduates can get away with such looks during academic recruiting, but such attire rarely leads to success in a corporate setting.

Interviewing Skills

Regardless of the position sought, be prepared: research the targeted university department or corporation ahead of time. The goal is to signal a genuine interest in employment with the entity in question. Bring an extra copy of the *CV* or résumé (even if email or hard copies have been sent earlier) and reprints of published papers already submitted before the interview. Having a business card can be useful, but for a student this isn't necessarily critical.

Recruiters allow for some nervousness on the part of candidates, but there is a limit. Fidgeting is a bad habit: tame it with practice. Solid eye contact as an indicator of a person's honesty, forthrightness and ability to communicate is emphasized in interviewer lore; learn to be comfortable looking directly at the interviewer. Before answering a question, listen carefully to the interviewer, take a moment to reflect and think, and *then* respond as precisely as possible.

An interview isn't the place to be overly modest; recount examples of skills and successes, but avoid coming across as arrogant or dismissive of others.

Many candidates discover they're able to overcome their shyness when they realize it's far simpler to be a bit more extroverted than to graduate without a job.

Preliminary Academic Job Search

There are basically two markets for those seeking academic employment. The most common is word of mouth, where a graduate's praises are verbally related to interested institutions by one's advisor. The second market involves a central conference which serves as a clearing house for many graduates in a particular field; these (typically) annual events give graduates an opportunity to interview with as many as several dozen potential employers over the course of several days.

Word of Mouth

As students busily prepare their job application packages, an informal network of professors is already discussing the most promising graduates. The advisors will begin the buzz by singing their praises to colleagues in other institutions. Recruiters at the best schools will immediately seek to set up interviews with the stars; interview spots are often limited, so other students find themselves competing for a dwindling number of interview opportunities.

Recruiters for less wealthy schools don't usually bother going after the stars, or do so half-heartedly, as they can neither compete on salary nor prestige. Thus, stars and non-stars are, to some extent, directed into two separate tiers: the highly recommended students to the wealthy schools, while those lacking ringing endorsements are funneled into other schools' interview slots. There are, of course, students between these two extremes, who may be able to find opportunities in both kinds of schools.

As the flurry of informal discussions takes place behind the scenes, students work with their advisors to identify institutions which appear to be interested in the student's work. Students then mail out application packages containing a copy of each academic paper completed to date, abstracts, several sealed reference letters, and an academic *CV*. Journal reprints should be included for any papers already published or forthcoming in a peer reviewed journal.

Students may expect to receive some feedback over the next few weeks; phone calls usually come from institutions interested in scheduling an on-site visit and presentation. Letters often inform applicants of rejections.

The willingness of the advisor to pick up the phone and "market" a student to her informal network of colleagues around the world may be the candidate's best, and only, shot at employment. The willingness and predisposition of a professor to do this on a student's behalf is therefore a critically important criterion in the original selection of an advisor.

Conference Format

There's usually one very large conference in the field, known to all as "the recruiting conference," for tenure-track positions. The formal conference is conducted according to schedule, while a parallel, full-fledged recruiting effort is organized to enable professors serving as selectors for their institution to attend the conference, and occasionally duck out and participate in interviews with candidates.

There is some strategy in preparing an interview schedule for such an event: set up one or two interviews with schools not among your top choices early on the first day, to serve as practice runs, to become more comfortable with the personal introduction, synopsis of the job market paper, and describing teaching interests. The main days of the conference are ideally set aside for interviews with institutions the student sees as more desirable. The last afternoon of the conference is also usually set aside for less desirable schools, as a fallback plan. After a dozen grueling interviews you may be tempted to cancel remaining ones. Don't do it! Recruiters may perceive last-day cancellations as a slight, a sign of your arrogance. The academic world is small and it doesn't pay to burn any bridges.

Follow Up

In the days and weeks following the interviews, recruiters may contact candidates directly with either a rejection, or with an invitation for a campus visit. Some recruiters may not call rejected candidates at all, leaving them to stew in uncertainty. In some cases students hear nothing for many weeks, conclude that they've been rejected, only to be contacted out of the blue and informed that they've made it to the next round. Some departments simply take (much) longer than others; in other cases, a department may place a candidate on a waiting list, pending progress with other candidates.

Students are well advised to follow up with recruiters a few weeks after the interviews have taken place. In one example, a dissertation committee member received a call from a recruiter at a school his student had applied to for employment. The recruiter indicated that he had not yet received a reference letter for the candidate from the candidate's dissertation advisor. The message was passed on to the student who subsequently inquired with his advisor, only to discover to the chagrin of both that the advisor had completely forgotten to send any reference letters for the student. This meant that all the student's applications had been incomplete. The red-faced and apologetic advisor expedited delivery of the letters. In this example, the candidate was lucky a recruiter was proactive.

A more reliable strategy is to follow up directly with each potential employer, ensuring that your application package is complete and making yourself available in the event any other questions or complications arise.

The Campus Visit

During a campus visit, a job candidate is usually expected to present his work and have one-on-one interviews with several faculty members; he can also expect to be taken out to lunch and/or dinner. The host institution will typically reimburse the candidate for all reasonable travel expenses. It's best to confirm this in advance of the visit.

Offers will be forthcoming if the student performs well during such visits and sufficiently impresses the faculty with her capabilities and passion.

What Recruiters Look For

Recruiters at academic institutions will ask questions in an effort to gauge the candidate's:

- Passion and commitment to the field. Will the candidate work hard and sustain productive energy over the long term, or will he lose interest in research and pursue other interests after a short time?

- Talent as a researcher. Is the candidate well-trained technically? Is he creative? Will he contribute to the prestige of the department?

- Ability to teach. Can the candidate do his share in maintaining or improving the department's teaching quality? Is he able and willing to teach courses others don't want to? Does he have non-academic experience which can help make classes more relevant or practical?

- Compatible professional interests, inclination and ability to collaborate. Will the candidate's presence open up opportunities for other faculty members to benefit directly? Will he collaborate willingly and enthusiastically, thereby assisting colleagues with their publishing success?

- Cultural fit. Will the candidate become a colleague who is pleasant to have around? Will he contribute to a constructive social atmosphere?

- Staying power. Does the candidate exhibit genuine commitment to the institution and is he interested in being there for the long-term?

- Manners. Does the candidate exhibit appropriate social skills?

The candidate should anticipate these and related questions, and have good answers prepared in advance. The candidate is well advised to recognize that he is being examined closely at all times—not just during a formal presentation or interview sessions. Meals and casual encounters with staff, even graduate students, are often viewed as opportunities to relax, but the candidate should not let his guard down at any time. Professional appearance and conduct are necessary at all times.

Almost everyone at the recruiting institution will ask for a brief description of the candidate's research interests and dissertation, usually upfront; the candidate must have something concise and intelligent to say. Candidates may also be asked what they know about the host institution. Items on the candidate's *CV*, especially unusual ones, often attract interest, which is why it's important to know one's *CV* inside out, and not include anything that can't be credibly explained. The usual corporate-style recruiting questions, such as, "Where do you see yourself in ten years?" or "Give an example of a failure which you turned to your advantage," and "Name your two greatest strengths and weaknesses" are often asked.

What Candidates Must Find Out During Campus Visits

A candidate should seek to have a number of questions answered during a campus recruiting visit. Not all questions are appropriate for all audiences, so use common sense to decide which of the locals to direct particular questions to: local graduate students, program administrators, junior professors, senior professors, the department chair, and possibly the dean of the school. Generally, the junior personnel (graduate students, junior faculty) will be more accessible than senior people (tenured faculty and administrators). Two of the candidate's most pressing objectives are likely to be:

- Exploring the theoretical and empirical research interests of faculty members and graduate students
- The nature and amount of financial support

There are, however, many other relevant questions to be explored.

Tenure Process:

- What are the requirements for tenure?
- Who has to weigh-in with approval at various levels?
- Is there a strict number of publications required to secure tenure?
- Do publications in different tiers of journals carry different weight in the tenure decision, and what are those weights?
- What are the timelines for tenure? How many years will it take to achieve tenure?
- How frequently do junior professors receive feedback on their performance?
- Has anyone recently failed to obtain tenure, and, if so, why?

Responsibilities to the Department:

- Will the candidate be required to sit on various committees (recruiting, student admissions)?
- Will the candidate be responsible for arranging a speaker or seminar series?

Career Considerations:

- What is the anticipated salary range?
- Is there a pension plan? How is it structured?
- How are annual salary increases determined?
- Are sabbaticals allowed? What are the conditions?
- What are the details of health care plans?
- Are professors allowed to engage in external consulting? Is this likely to be an option? Do other professors from the department engage in such activities?
- What are the intellectual property right conventions with respect to property generated while under the employ of the university?

Financial State of the Department and Future Plans:

- What are the big picture plans for the department (expansion of student body, additional faculty, or new facilities)?
- Is a move to a different location likely?
- Are there any expected cutbacks looming?
- Is the department operating within budget?
- Is any of the department's funding in danger of drying up?

Resource Availability:

- How modern and accessible are computing facilities and support staff?
- Which software packages are available?
- Are graduate students available for teaching and/or research assistantships?
- How large and modern is laboratory or studio space (as relevant, depending on the field of study)?

- How much funding is available for computers, travel to conferences, hiring part-time workers, or compensation of research subjects?
- Is there assistance available for grant writing?
- Are there funds available to purchase important inputs to the research process, such as databases and research materials?
- What are library facilities like? Are they well-stocked with relevant volumes and periodicals?

The Student Body:

- What is the number of students at each level (undergraduate, master's, doctoral)?
- What is the quality of students at each level?
- How does the motivation of the average student compare to the motivation of students at other institutions?
- How successful are undergraduate students at securing jobs?
- How successful are master's students at securing jobs?
- How successful are PhD students in securing academic jobs?

Teaching Responsibilities:

- How many classes are professors required to teach?
- How large are the classes?
- How frequently is course material expected to be updated?
- Is it possible to inherit class notes from former professors?
- Will teaching include doctoral courses?
- Is it possible to be involved in executive education?
- Is summer teaching expected?
- How is summer teaching compensated?
- How is teaching quality evaluated?
- Are any courses particularly difficult to staff?

- Are any specific teaching methods emphasized? Are any discouraged?

Living Conditions and Logistics:

- What is the quality of schools and daycare facilities?
- Do professors' children qualify for tuition waivers if they enroll at the school or any of its affiliated programs?
- What are the crime levels on and around the campus, and in the relevant residential neighborhoods?
- What health care facilities are available?
- Is there on-campus parking?
- What food facilities are available on or near campus?
- Is there a faculty club, and, if so, what services are available?
- Are relocation expenses covered?
- Where do most professors live?

Human Interaction Quality:

- How well do graduate students interact with each other?
- How well do faculty members interact with each other?
- How well do faculty members interact with graduate students? Is the former group accessible to the latter? Is the atmosphere one of mutual respect? Do they seek out each other's company?

Recruiting Process:

- How many people are being interviewed?
- When will final decisions be made?
- How much time does the candidate have to make his acceptance decision?

Some students begin employment prior to successful defense of the PhD; in these cases it's important to establish some ground rules with the prospective employer, including:

- Will the employer make any allowances (e.g., reduced teaching load) while the candidate completes the PhD?
- When will the tenure clock start ticking? As soon as the ABD arrives on campus, or only once the PhD is received?
- What happens in the event the candidate fails to successfully defend the dissertation?

Nonacademic Positions

This book is specifically directed at helping people decide whether the academic world is for them. Non-academic (corporate and government) jobs are, however, legitimate outcomes for graduates of academic programs, and are addressed below. Before doing so, it's necessary first to address the possibility that these non-academic positions are being pursued involuntarily: that is, because the graduate is unable to find academic employment.

Seeking Nonacademic Positions Involuntarily

Students who involuntarily seek non-academic jobs have an important hurdle to overcome—the trauma of seeing their aspirations for an academic life destroyed. To understand their bitterness one must imagine being in their shoes, toiling over the course of a decade of university education (assuming a four-year bachelor's degree, a two-year master's, and a four-year PhD), surviving all the ups and downs of examinations, writing and defending a dissertation, committing emotionally to accept all the hard work and struggle and sacrifice, then suddenly being told they have no future in their chosen field. Anyone placed in such circumstances might be embittered. Some feel victimized at being unfairly judged or may question their own competence. Either conclusion may affect their confidence and self-esteem for years to come.

The biggest challenge in this predicament is to avoid carrying this bitterness directly into a corporate job search. The more intense one's negative emotions, the more likely these are to adversely affect the search. This is especially unfortunate as there can be significant benefits to joining a corporation. Reassessing the situation objectively, including recognition of better compensation and other benefits of corporate positions, can lead to a healthier approach to finding satisfying employment.

Corporate Jobs

Tens of thousands of new PhDs graduate each year; many settle into academic positions (including government research laboratories and think tank roles), and thousands more seek employment in corporate entities. Those who go the corporate route do so either voluntarily—because they are more interested in the private sector—or, as discussed above, they do so involuntarily because they are unable to find employment in the academic world.

Corporate jobs generally mean higher salaries than those available for similar skill sets in an academic setting: salaries in readily commercialized fields, such as engineering, biosciences, business, and law often equate to or exceed the compensation for full professors. There are exceptions for professors who write bestsellers or are greatly in demand as consultants.

Business also offers greater diversity of roles to experience, which some people consider an important source of stimulus over the course of a career.

On the downside, it's a fairly common observation by former academics that corporate positions lack intellectual stimulation: there is also far less autonomy or freedom to pursue one's own agenda because the work is entirely dictated by the firm's commercial orientation.

Business employment is subject to the vagaries of the marketplace, just as academic employment is subject to funding cuts. Regardless of individual talents, during a downturn employees may face a significant probability of being "downsized" (fired), or, as it's more fashionably referred to these days, "right-sized," which still means fired!

PhD graduates bring highly desired skills to corporate employment. They should recognize and emphasize their ability to think critically, and their discipline in assessing evidence objectively—separating presumption from fact. Another important strength many PhDs possess is their ability to look at themselves very critically. Critical self-evaluation can often be humbling, but those who survive it learn important lessons, including graceful acceptance of external criticism and an inclination for constructive criticism of oneself and others. These are immensely powerful skill sets.

Government Jobs

Government is, to some extent, a hybrid of academic and corporate attributes: its institutions typically have a corporate-like structure, but many functions are actually closer to the pure research model. Government research positions often allow staff to devote themselves to research without teaching duties: some government agencies produce excellent research and are well-respected by the academic community—the National Institutes of Health (NIH), The Centers for Disease Control (CDC), and the U.S. Federal Reserve, for example. Government positions offer good job security, even during rough stretches in the broader economy, but may come at the expense of the size of the paycheck.

On the downside, government institutions are often associated with bureaucracy and, at times, mediocrity and politicizing scientific theories and findings.

Why is it Such a Big Deal to Leave the Ivory Tower?

Even those who pursue nonacademic positions voluntarily may have fears about leaving the comforts of the ivory tower. Some of the most prevalent are:

- Fear of the unknown. There is a natural reluctance to leave behind the familiarity and comforts of autonomous research and an exciting intellectual atmosphere; the prospect of leaving the protected cocoon to enter another culture where one has very little standing can be very intimidating.

- The inability to come back to academia. The literature progresses so quickly, in some fields an absence of just two years makes a successful return virtually impossible: the decision to leave academia is often seen as a one-way street. Some former academics make a comeback as adjunct professors, but in almost-exclusively teaching roles, as it's very difficult to get back to rigorous research after an extended absence from the field. There are exceptions. For example, an economist at the U.S. Federal Reserve may be welcomed into an academic research position.

- Concern about being perceived as "selling out" the purity of academic pursuits. There are those who believe the rigor and purity of academics are sacrosanct. One interpretation of accepting employment outside research and teaching is that you are leaving all that is true and pure behind to pursue the almighty dollar. This view is often emphasized by those who stay behind—namely one's professors and fellow graduates. After working closely for so many years, it's easy to allow them to make you feel guilty or doubt your own motives. Don't let this happen. Academe is extremely insular, and occasionally narrow-minded: there are many other worthy and satisfying career options available.

Why Do Academics Often Fail Outside Academia?

While some former academics thrive in the private sector, others experience significant difficulties. The reasons are often that academics:

- May have difficulty relating to lay people. The inability to connect intellectually or empathetically may be attributed to two causes: (1) they don't realize they are talking over other people's heads, and (2) they don't take the time to relate to others because they feel it's beneath them to have to explain "the obvious" to people they consider less intelligent. Obviously, neither of these is constructive; number one is at least easier to fix.

- Manifest a fascination for fine detail. Esoteric "facts" are appropriate in academic settings, but in time- and goal-oriented business environments detail may be considered tangential, trivial, and a waste of resources: while colleagues are moving on, former academics are revving up for heated debate. This brings us back to the refrain "academics debate fiercely because there is nothing at stake." But there *is* something at stake—opportunity cost. Every minute spent on irrelevant arguments is another minute not spent more productively.

- Exhibit a lack of urgency. Formulating and articulating sound answers to problems and moving on is often critical in competitive marketplaces: academics abhor a rush to judgment without sufficient scientific data, so former academics may fail to act promptly enough. A fast, reasonably accurate answer is often better than a perfect, but too-late answer: one can be reasonably successful by making solid decisions without expending significant resources.

- Lack social skills. Eccentric and irreverent behavior permissible in an academic setting can be interpreted as highly offensive in other settings. Failure to control emotions and/or communicate diplomatically is a failure to behave acceptably.

- Fail to merge theory and practice. Without this ability to use theoretical knowledge to solve business, engineering, or other real problems, even those with creative genius and monumental intellect find it hard to properly inform and influence others, significantly reducing the value they bring to an organization.

- Fail to exhibit poise. While not unique to academics, the insular and tolerant academic environment occasionally leaves former academics without the emotional tools to handle certain types of adversity.

Chapter 8: Academics' Contributions to Society

"All truth passes through three stages. First, it is ridiculed. Second, it is violently opposed. Third, it is accepted as being self-evident." -Arthur Schopenhauer (1788-1860)

"I have not failed. I've just found 10,000 ways that won't work." -Thomas Alva Edison (1847-1931)

In his book, *Guns, Germs and Steel*, Jared Diamond stresses the importance of technological progress to a society's prosperity and security. Given the importance of experimentation, scientific discovery, and technological innovation to our society, we all share the responsibility for asking who safeguards our society's scientific endeavors. The answer: the academic community.

The focus of this chapter is on academia's role in safeguarding and maintaining the integrity of the scientific process, protecting freedom of thought and expression, and educating future generations of scientists.

Safeguards for patents and intellectual property are not addressed explicitly here; while such legal infrastructure is undoubtedly relevant, the focus in this book is those factors under the direct control of the academic community.

Rigorous Research: Maintaining the Integrity of the Scientific Process

Academics play a critical role in society by zealously defending the integrity of the scientific process. This encompasses proper collection of evidence, model and study design, model and study testing, documenting all activities, and accurately interpreting results. Without this discipline, one would be unable to gauge the relevance—or believability—of any purported research results.

This discipline is critical because there is always the possibility a particular research activity may be flawed—due to either honest mistakes or sinister motives. Governments, corporations, and individuals have, throughout the ages, attempted to subvert research for political or financial gain, or both.

Society looks to the academic community to provide the expertise and rigor needed to protect consumers or citizens who are ignorant of health, economic, political, and social dangers. When corporations and governments rely on their own credentialed academics to support their positions, establishing whether a particular piece of research is flawed or manipulated can be extremely difficult. Recent research in psychology has shed some light on how easy it is for government or special interest groups to deflect rigorous scientific conclusions, to the detriment of society. One specific example shows how public opinion can be swayed by nonexperts on the subject of climate change.[2] The academic community has concluded quite definitively that climate change has been caused, at least partially, by humans. Many media reports have provided this conclusion. Yet, much of society believes the evidence is, at best, questionable, because when media reports come out, they are often followed by counterarguments presented by special interest groups. The psychological study alluded to above has shown that a 45-second opposing view, following a televised report establishing the existence of climate change and human culpability, is sufficient to counteract the enlightening effect on viewers. Thus, despite having no scientific evidence to debunk the role of humans in climate change, special interest groups can alter an important message by planting seeds of doubt. These obfuscations serve the purposes of special interest groups, but can pose a real danger to society. Thus, the academic community often must work hard both to collect scientific evidence, and, subsequently, carry its message to the rest of society.

Clearly, there can be many gray areas in the struggle to determine whether research on any topic is sufficiently rigorous. This section explores the important safeguards for which the scientific community is responsible.

Performing Sound Research

Good research requires broad understanding of the bigger picture, a good measure of intuition, rigorous methodology applied by appropriately trained technicians, natural curiosity about a particular subject, and often, a team effort. More brains and pairs of eyes and ears are more observant than one brain or pair of eyes and ears. Group work can efficiently bring complementary skill sets to bear—especially important in an increasingly specialized and sophisticated research environment.

A prevailing myth is that good research can only be conducted in good universities; this false belief arises from the observation that the better schools are wealthier, allowing them to hire smarter people, and surround them with the best facilities and materials. Another opinion is that the most influential journals are dominated by faculty from the best schools, and entry into this "club" is difficult for outsiders. It's an inescapable fact that the wealthier schools can provide better facilities to their faculty; their prestige does help them recruit talented people. But better facilities and talented people do not automatically mean everyone else's efforts are doomed to failure. Anyone with a good head on their shoulders can perform good research by adhering to the scientific method.

One can think of the scientific method as the framework for responsible research: the most important features of scientific claims are their reliability, validity, and level of significance; there is also the need to distinguish between *cause* and *effect*.

Reliability and Validity

Reliability applies to the *repeatability* of the reported results, in response to the question, "Can reported results be replicated by following the process documented by the original researcher(s)?"

Validity refers to whether the reported results do, in fact, apply to the scientist's claim. For example, a scientist may claim he's discovered cold fusion in a test tube and present photographs of a frothing test tube. The claim is *reliable* if others, in independent labs, can *replicate* the documented result(s). The procedure is *valid* if it is determined to truly lead to a fusion reaction, as claimed. There is always the danger that the frothing bubbles reported in the original claim, and replicated by others, are not due to a fusion reaction, but some other chemical reaction. In such cases, the original claims would be considered invalid.

Is it always possible to set up real experiments to solve any question? Emphatically, no! The less controllable the situation, the more difficult it is to prepare a valid and reliable test environment. On the other hand, some experiments can be performed with astounding validity and reliability. Just think of what can be done with advanced laboratory clean rooms: identical test tubes can be filled with identical contents, under precisely controlled temperature and humidity; even a very slight alteration in one chemical compound injected into each test tube can lead to highly measurable, distinct differences. Some fields of science have the luxury of using such highly controlled environments for experimentation, particularly the natural and life sciences (physics, chemistry, biology).

Other fields of study, such as the social sciences (e.g., psychology, economics, etc.), are far less controllable. How does one accurately predict the course of human emotion, or control for the movements of the stock market, with all its intricate moving parts? Research efforts in the fields of humanities (English, history, art) are even less controllable. How does one devise an experiment to determine whether Van Gogh would have painted better or worse if he had his ear back on? Would Beethoven have been a better composer if he'd had better hearing?

These differences in attainable control and precision are the reasons the natural sciences are often referred to as the "hard" or precise sciences, while the humanities and social sciences are considered the "soft" or imprecise sciences. The particular ambiguity in the field of economics has led to it being considered the "dismal" science.

The scope for practical implementation of scientific results from different fields also varies significantly. Results of highly controllable biology experiments can lead to very quick implementation. Once a vaccine is discovered and replicated, it can be available within days or weeks to a large population, and the effects on the population can be understood well in advance of inoculations. In less-precise fields, it may take far longer for theory to be converted into practical policy. Formulation of a new theory of the effects of government spending on growth out of a recession may be just the beginning of a decades-long process. The lack of controls in testing such a theory will mean many heated debates and an agonizing road to gaining acceptance for the idea.

Significance

Significance is a measure of how *meaningful* a particular result is. Perhaps an intuitive example is the best way to understand this concept. Consider a new manager or coach of a sports team: her first task is to assess the scoring abilities of three players, using an objective measure. One reasonable option would be to look at each player's scoring output from last season. The coach decides to use a standardized measure: number of points scored divided by number of minutes played. Based on this measure, she immediately notes one of three players, Player A, stands head and shoulders above the rest. But, on closer inspection, Player A has only played 20 minutes the entire season. Does she believe this player will maintain the same measure of points-per-minute throughout the entire season? How *meaningful* is this result? Because the playing time is so short, the result cannot be taken as highly meaningful, so she moves on to examine the other two players. Each has played more than twenty games, logged over 1,000 minutes of play over the season; their points-per-minute statistics are much more robust. Player B has scored 1.01 points per 100 minutes, while Player C has scored 1.05 points per 100 minutes. Is player C clearly the best offensive weapon the team has?

It's impossible to say so with certainty: many other factors, such as the effects of weather on the games played, the varying composition of the team fielded for each game, and the quality of the opponent guarding Players A, B, and C throughout the season have not been considered. Because there is no cut-and-dry, correct answer to the question who is the best player, significance is typically quoted as a statistical measure with some tolerance, or confidence interval. *Significance* often quantifies the probability that the result is sufficiently unusual to be seen as *meaningful*.

In the example above, the results of 1.01 and 1.05 seem very close, but a statistical analysis may show that even this small difference is highly significant, or unusual. If so, it is possible to conclude that Player C's score of 1.05 does place the player in a more elite group. In the event a statistical analysis concludes that a difference of 0.04 between scores is very typical, it would not be possible in this example to statistically distinguish Player C from Player B.

Correlation and Causality

Correlation is a measure of the tendency of certain pairs of observations to move in a related, or unrelated, fashion. A high, or positive, correlation between two observations means they tend to move together. A low, or negative, correlation indicates they tend to move in opposite directions. An example is education level and future income. Studies show there is a high positive correlation between these two measures: people with higher education levels tend to earn higher incomes over the course of their careers.

As with any statistical measure, correlation must be critically examined before conclusions are drawn. For a variety of reasons, including experimental errors, the time periods chosen for analysis, and bias in the underlying population, correlation measures may be misleading. Consider the example of education and income, and suppose the correlation measure was generated for sophisticated quantitative analysts ("quants") working on Wall Street. Such a collection of people would exhibit advanced degrees in mathematics and physics (high education) as well as typical Wall Street salaries (high incomes): positive correlation. Next consider a very different population: social workers toiling in inner city neighborhoods. In this case there would be advanced sociology degrees (high education), coupled with typical salaries paid by government agencies and non-profit organizations (low income), yielding a negative correlation between income and education. Thus, two very different populations exhibit very different correlations. It would be a mistake to automatically assume that a correlation measure based on one of the populations applies to the other, or for that matter, any other population.

While high correlation means that two variables are related, *causality* is a stronger statement that says not only are two variables related, but one *causes* the other. A major pitfall when analyzing experimental results or observations is the common assumption that *correlation* is the same as *causality*. In the current example, one may hypothesize that higher education *causes* higher income in subsequent years. That is, higher education allows people to obtain better-paying jobs and receive more promotions, leading to higher compensation.

The example involving causality between education and earnings is intuitively appealing. Generally, however, we cannot assume causality just because there is evidence of correlation. Logical thinking and the integrity of the academic process require us to be more precise. Here is an example emphasizing that one cannot blindly measure correlation and assume causality. Consider a visit to the local supermarket, observing shoppers' obesity levels and the contents of their shopping carts. The objective is to measure whether there is a relationship between the two variables: obesity and food choice. The experiment yield: obese shoppers tend to have more diet food in their carts. Mathematically, this observation suggests a positive correlation between the two. An effort to impose causality here may lead the researcher to conclude that diet food causes obesity—a nonsensical result. Clearly, here is an example where correlation between two variables isn't the same as causality. To emphasize this point, let's revisit the earlier example, relating income to education: an analogously flawed conclusion may be that high income (in future) causes more education (in the past).

In the examples above, it's easy to critically examine the causality assumption and dismiss it; however, there are many other situations where such clarity is not so readily available. Suppose, for example, that in the education and income example, we had not specified *future* income, but stated it more generally as a correlation between income and education. As before, intuition supports the argument that higher education is associated with (or causes) higher income. But now, one could also argue that the presence of higher income (early on) allows a person more time and money to afford more education: income causing education.

When it comes to correlation and causality, an experimenter must measure and interpret carefully. Disciplined and logical thinking is, therefore, extremely important; the academic community is responsible for imposing and maintaining such discipline.

Protecting Freedom of Thought, Opinion, Exploration, Expression and Speech

"Every debate about universities must include academic freedom—an oft-overlooked core value requisite for effective teaching and research." - Philip G. Altbach, in "Academic Freedom in a Global Context: 21st Century Challenges," *The NEA 2007 Almanac of Higher Education.*

Consider the following statements:

1. The sun and the moon are not gods—they are merely two celestial bodies among an infinite number of such bodies.
2. The earth isn't flat—it's round.
3. The earth revolves around the sun.

These statements may appear entirely self-evident today; so obvious, they're trivial. Yet a few centuries ago, expressing such sentiments publicly often meant death.

It is possible today to recognize the truths listed above because brave scholars spoke out many years ago, challenging incorrect, but established, views. Their challenge, motivated by a commitment to objectivity and scientific integrity, frequently led to excommunication, torture, and death.

Remarkable as it may seem, such repression still takes place in the twenty-first century. There is a very high correlation between a society repressing scientific theories and repressing freedom of speech, expression, exploration, thought, and development. Thus, it's critically important for any society to have courageous individuals willing to speak out in defense of these freedoms: these individuals often pay a price for such statements, but inspire people around them with the logic and decency of their claims, gaining momentum for change and reform.

Academics can become a powerful force when they unite, especially when they inspire large student bodies to follow their lead. Powerful student movements have reshaped our world. Consider the revolution in Iran, Berkeley's Vietnam War demonstrations, protests in favor of democracy in China and budding efforts in Arab countries. The power of intellectual motivation is immense, and can support constructive or destructive agendas.

The potential power of an academic institution attracts those who would hijack it for their own purposes. When institutions of higher education deviate from their mission and become indoctrination centers, rather than places of enlightenment, knowledge is distorted in the service of pernicious influences. In the dawn of the twenty-first century, the effects of fanatical religious indoctrination of vulnerable students, delivered within institutions claiming to be committed to education, were made frighteningly clear.

Recent and ancient history clearly show that, in most cases of real academic institutions being usurped for such dark purposes, there are preliminary warning signs. The perpetrators are often government institutions, seeking to cloak authoritarian ideology and dogma as social and economic theory, a movement necessary to social progress, or, more extremely, the survival of a nation. Brave individuals, often faculty members who see the fallacies and dangers inherent in the ideology, attempt to stem the dark forces threatening their campus. They challenge misleading or inappropriate course content; they call for open-mindedness and tolerance; they put themselves in the line of fire. Their noble efforts bring reprisals to silence them: they may be subjected to threats, dismissal, imprisonment, corporal and capital punishment. Without help, these individual scholars and their overall cause is doomed. The academic community's strength is in its ability to appeal to moderates: the overall population has a collective responsibility to support the brave efforts of these individuals, allying with them to create a mobilized community which cannot be ignored.

Educating Future Generations

The third major contribution of academics to society—after their rigorous research yields discoveries—is to make these discoveries accessible and ultimately useful, by bringing findings and conclusions to the masses. Scholars' knowledge is of no use if it cannot be successfully relayed to others. A frequent mistake by arrogant academics—assuming anyone who can't follow what they're doing is stupid, and, therefore, unworthy—is the worst sort of attitude, held only by those academics who mistakenly believe the universe revolves around them. A true scholar recognizes the power she possesses to enlighten others, and acts responsibly as a conveyor of knowledge.

Some insight into the rot in our system of higher education may be found in a book compiled by Shepherd College History Professor Anders Henriksson,[3] which contains the following passages, found in college students' history papers:

1. Judyism was the first monolithic religion. It had one big God named "Yahoo." Old Testament profits include Moses, Amy and Confucius, who believed in Fidel Piety.

2. Victims of the Black Death grew boobs on their necks. Death rates exceeded 100 percent in some towns.

3. History, a record of things left behind by past generations, started in 1815. Thus, we should try to view historical times as the behind of the present. This gives incite into the anals of the past.

4. Zorroastrologism was founded by Zorro. This was a duelist religion. The three gods were "Good," "Bad," and "Indifferent." These beliefs later resurfaced among the Manatees.

No doubt some elitist readers have had their chuckle and muttered to themselves this is just what they'd expect from the small colleges littering the mid-American landscape. But our leading university students are not exempt. According to Debbie Schlussel:

> In 2000, the Center for Survey Research and Analysis at the University of Connecticut administered a 34-question high-school-level American history test to college seniors at 55 top colleges and universities. Nearly 80 percent failed, including those from Ivy League schools like Harvard and Princeton.[4]

Schlussel isn't the only one concerned with the efficacy of our system of higher education. Similar concerns have infiltrated the top echelons of our most revered institutions of higher learning. Even our academic icons seem to be dropping the ball on education. A 1998 article by Sharon Dolovich[5] discusses why students at one of the nation's most prestigious schools—the Harvard Law School—end up "subdued, withdrawn, and uncertain of their self-worth." During a recent (2008) discussion, Dolovich, at time of writing a Professor of Law at UCLA, opined that while the Harvard Law School environment has changed for the better over the past decade, her original observations still capture some important aspects of the law school experience for many students, and that the phenomenon appears to be present to varying degrees at other law schools.

One can only conclude, with significant disappointment in the system, that if the most privileged students can become so downtrodden, rather than being confident and poised, something must be wrong.

The aspiring PhD student may wonder why the focus in this section is on the problems within undergraduate programs. After all, this book is about graduate education, so why all the fuss about some poorly educated undergraduates? The reason is very simple: the PhD is a license to teach and mentor these undergraduates; great responsibility comes with the license. Most graduate students see their role as researcher; not enough of them recognize the importance of their role as educator and mentor.

Chapter 9: Institutions of Higher Learning

To the dean—who does well despite his faculties. - Anonymous

In the previous chapter, I emphasized the important roles academics play in safeguarding our society. The next question to explore is where do academics work, meet, and collaborate? The answer is, traditionally, academics are employed by a college or university. In addition, academics may be employed by think tanks, government institutions, research institutes, and/or corporations. The emphasis of this book is on universities.

What is a University?

According to Wikipedia, "the word *university* is derived from the Latin *universitas magistrorum et scholarium*, roughly meaning 'community of masters and scholars'." Universities are institutions devoted to research and education, and have the authority to grant academic degrees at various levels (bachelor, master, and doctorate), often across a broad array of subjects.

In most societies, universities are the centers of thought, intellectual leadership, and scholarship. The academic community is often thought to be relatively insulated from politics and commercial interests. Thus, academics are often viewed as more objective than non-academics. In reality, universities can be highly politicized, although on the whole, it's fair to say that tolerance for pluralism and open-mindedness are relatively more abundant in academic settings than elsewhere in most societies.

Public universities are government-funded; private ones are often independent of public funding and associated state influence. Most universities offer degree programs in several Faculties or departments, which may include the social and natural sciences, humanities, engineering, business, law, education, and medicine.

What is a Faculty?

A Faculty is a major division of a university, and may include a number of departments. An example is the Faculty of Arts or Humanities, which may contain literature, art, art history, history, and music departments. The Faculty of Engineering may contain civil, mechanical, chemical, and electrical engineering departments.

In colloquial use, "faculty" is a term often used to refer to the professors—members of the faculty—within a department, division, or entire university. In this book, "Faculty" (uppercase) is used to refer to the academic division, while "faculty" (lowercase) refers to the group of professors.

The Officers of a University

A university is led by a team of scholars and managers, responsible for all the research, education, and operational functions of the institution. A number of prominent roles on a university campus are described below.

President, Rector, Chancellor

The president, rector and chancellor [6] titles may be used interchangeably to refer to a university's highest ranking official. The most common title in the United States is "president," while "rector" is common in Europe. The analogous role in business is Chief Executive Officer. Chancellor or president is an honorary or ceremonial role, without any real managerial power, in many universities.

Provost

The provost is typically a senior academic administrator, thought of as the Chief Academic Officer; the precise role and seniority may vary, depending on the country and university system. Often, the provost is the second-highest ranking academic official, reporting directly to the president (or chancellor/rector) and the board. In his or her capacity as highest-ranking academic officer, the provost may be responsible for a university's research and academic personnel, including the deans of all faculties, schools, or colleges, as well as academic support units, such as admissions, academic facilities, libraries, student services, and information technology. These duties are handled by a variety of senior- and middle-level managers, some of whom are described below.

Dean

A dean is typically the head of a university department or Faculty, and often reports to a high-ranking university official such as the provost. In addition to deans of academic departments, other operating units of a university may be headed by a dean, such as the Dean of Students or Student Affairs.

Professor

Professor: A man who talks in his students' sleep. - Anonymous

According to Douglas Harper's *Online Etymology Dictionary*, a professor is a "person who professes to be an expert in some art or science; teacher of highest rank."[7]

Most new faculty members begin their careers as assistant professors. Once they attain tenure, they qualify for an associate professorship. Finally, the most senior faculty members may attain full professor status. Retired, tenured professors may remain associated with a university as emeritus professors. Professors who don't have tenure and aren't in tenure-track positions are often referred to as adjunct, or visiting, professors.

Board

The board is responsible for overall governance of a university. Equivalent terms are Governing Board, Board of Trustees, the Board of Regents, or the corporate Board of Directors. Public university board members may be appointed by a government body. Boards often include wealthy and influential people with academic, business, or government backgrounds. The university president is typically selected by the board and may be dismissed by the board. A board typically numbers a dozen or so people.

Administration of a University

Many people have the mistaken notion that universities are home to just two types of people: students and professors. In this simplified world-view, students study, play, and party, while professors teach and undertake research. Universities are, of course, far more complex institutions: some are as large and sophisticated as small cities, and employ thousands of clerks, facilities managers, maintenance personnel, security experts, finance, legal and accounting professionals, purveyors of food, waste management staff, and the list goes on. Leading these legions of university employees, as well as the professor and student populations, requires managers and administrators at all levels. Historically, many of these roles have been filled by members of the academic community.

In a world of steadily eroding public funding, rising tuition costs, neglected facilities and budget cuts, university administrators are called on to make difficult, painful decisions. The decisions often have little to do with academics, as a university's viability depends on many other functions: finance and budgeting, fund-raising, construction, building maintenance—including classrooms, athletic facilities, and student housing—managing cafeterias and other eating establishments, and coordinating the university's affairs with adjacent communities. Often, this means restricting availability of scholarships, grants, and other forms of financial aid, determining which academic programs are to be given preference, which may have to be under-funded or even shut down, and limiting salaries and benefits of employees and graduate students.

Many academics are keenly focused on their research, on unlocking the mysteries of the universe, and have absolutely no interest in anything else. They avoid administrative departmental chair positions and deanships at all costs, as they often see the required two- or three-year commitment as a period of bureaucratic and administrative hell, an exile from their main priority—research. Sometimes, when there are no volunteers for chair positions, these unwanted jobs are foisted upon new tenure recipients, who often don't want the job, and don't have the required skills in the first place. Under such circumstances, departments often sink into some period of relative dysfunction.

But some academics voluntarily seek administrative and managerial positions, pursuing these career paths for a variety of reasons, including a genuine desire to make a positive change within a department, or to serve more political ambitions.

Rank-and-file professors and students often form a negative view of these decision-makers, who are perceived as the "bad guys" holding the purse strings. Making matters worse, those who take on managerial duties often leave behind research and teaching duties, and are occasionally perceived as having turned their backs on the purest aspects of academe in favor of political gain.

In their defense, many of these managers do their best, but are ill-equipped for their jobs. Management requires far more than an academic publication record: many former academics find managerial and administrative skills impossible to master, and are unable to make and execute decisions properly.

Battles for senior administrative positions can be quite heated. Increasingly, there is more at stake than prestige for the most senior players. The high demand for skilled administrators who can win and retain the trust of their academic communities has led to steady salary inflation; today, many university presidents command very generous pay packages and benefits. A recent article by Jonathan Glater explored this trend based on a survey by *The Chronicle of Higher Education*. Here is an excerpt:

> The latest survey of 853 colleges, universities and specialized schools for subjects like medicine found that 112 paid their presidents at least $500,000. And it showed the upward spiral of compensation occurring in public institutions as well as private ones, with 42 presidents of public colleges earning $500,000 or more compared with the 23 reported in last year's survey.[8]

One Ivy League professor made headlines in the 1990s in his bid to become chair of his department: university administrators refused to allow him to hold the position because he was dating one of his graduate students. In response, he argued that the bureaucrats should stay out of his personal life. He was ultimately allowed to serve because no one else wanted the job.

Graduate students are well-advised to keep in mind most of the thousands of administrative staff members—secretaries, clerks, physical grounds maintenance personnel, and information technology specialists—who often get no attention or recognition at all. While their roles may seem far less prestigious and glamorous than full professors, department chairs and deans, their efforts are necessary to keep large universities in business. Academics (professors and students) often underestimate the importance of these staff members, exhibiting dismissive attitudes toward them. These attitudes can backfire when a real crisis strikes, or when a staff person's underappreciated skills at negotiating Byzantine procedures make the difference between getting approval for conference attendance, grant applications, travel budgets or not.

Chapter 10: Life in the Ivory Tower

"Let Schoolmasters puzzle their brain
With Grammar and nonsense and learning;
Good liquor, I stoutly maintain,
Gives genius a better discerning."
- Oliver Goldsmith (1730-1774)

The Two Pillars of Academe: Research and Education

The world of academe revolves around two main pillars: research and education. Classically, an institution of higher learning is expected to pursue excellence in both. In reality, education usually gives way to research, one consequence of the well-known academic imperative: "Publish or perish!"

Research

"Research is what I'm doing when I don't know what I'm doing." - Wernher Von Braun (1912-1977)

The purpose of research is to add to society's knowledge by delving into the universe's mysteries. Discoveries lead to a greater understanding of the world and allow us to harness—or at least predict—some of the forces of nature, improving the lives of all people. Intensive research efforts are among the academic community's critical contributions to society.

A distinction is often made between *pure* research and *applied* research. *Pure* research is also referred to as fundamental research; it focuses on examination of basic or fundamental theories or laws of nature, including physical and biological properties of the universe, its flora and fauna. *Applied* research involves the use or extension of academic theories, methodologies, and techniques for specific social or commercial purposes. Given the proximity of applied research to commercial applications, it often benefits greatly from access to funding from corporations, while pure research is typically more reliant on government grants. Consequently, from an academic's perspective, there is usually more funding available for applied research projects than there is for pure research.

Globally, large numbers of scholars engage in intense efforts to delve ever deeper into their chosen fields; in these research processes, they produce terabytes of data—raw, analyzed, written up, some of it polished for publication. Some of these efforts yield quality research: but, it's not uncommon for some research to appear to be meaningless. The challenge, of course, is to determine how and whether anyone should be allowed to determine what is, and what is not, worthless. As the saying goes, "One man's brilliant research may be another's folly."

The two issues involved above (the freedom to undertake any research versus oversight or censorship) may never truly be reconciled. Poor research must be tolerated because the open environment which allows for poor research is a necessary and critical ingredient for good research. As soon as someone decides to censor another's work, research freedom is negatively affected. One person's creativity and out-of-the-box thinking is another's heresy or stupidity. Yet, so often, it's the person who dares to challenge conventional thinking who contributes most significantly. Sadly, many such contributions are only appreciated well after the contributor's lifetime.

The uncertain, winding path of progress in research is well-described by Oliver Sacks in *Uncle Tungsten: Memories of a Chemical Boyhood*:

> It was evident that the history of science was anything but a straight and logical series. That it leapt about, split, converged, diverged, took off at tangents, repeated itself, got into jams and concerns.

Education

"I have never let my schooling interfere with my education." - Mark Twain (1835-1910)

It would be difficult to find an economist, sociologist, demographer, or humanist who would deny that education is critically important to every person on the planet. Among other benefits, education is one of the most important factors in improving a nation's standard of living, as well as reducing high birth rates and violence. Without proper education, scientists' important new discoveries cannot be understood and embraced by others for the betterment of society.

While technology, such as the Internet, has changed education over the past two decades, a key aspect remains in place: the university or college campus (whether virtual or physical) remains the acknowledged provider of higher education. To drive home the importance of education to our society, consider its economic impact on two dimensions: one, it allows people to be more productive, thereby adding much value to society. Two, it's a huge export industry.

Publish or Perish!

In principle, the two pillars of the academic world—research and education—should coexist in balanced fashion. In practice, however, research is often the dominant factor which drives much of the academic world. Good researchers receive far more prestige and financial compensation than good educators; tenure decisions hinge on research productivity more than any other component. Newly minted professors dream about making the world's next big discovery, not about facing a hungover class of undergraduates on a Monday morning. The academic community's highest honor—the Nobel prize—is given for research contributions, not for teaching prowess.

The building blocks of a researcher's career are publications in peer reviewed journals. These are described below.

What Is a Journal?

A *journal* is a *periodical* containing *articles* written by members of a particular academic *field*. Some examples of fields are economics, political science, aeronautical engineering, French literature, immunology, and exercise physiology. Journals serve as discussion forums for thousands of academic communities; they also contain announcements of events such as conferences, and in some cases include advertisements and job listings within the field.

Scholars may submit articles to a journal for publication. Peer reviewed journals have a number of established academics on their editorial boards. The editors read and review submitted articles: their responsibility is to decide whether the submission is appropriate, given the journal's stated specialty, and whether the submission is of sufficient quality to be printed in an upcoming issue of the journal. When the editors are not sufficiently familiar with the subject matter, they may ask others to help with the review process.

Several different journals may exist within a given field; usually, some have less rigorous acceptance standards than others. The most rigorous and selective are the most prestigious.

Success in academics is generally judged by the number of peer reviewed publications a scholar has amassed. Publications in the best journals are highly prized. Generally, a few publications in the best journal outweigh more numerous publications in minor, or fringe journals. The distinction is so significant some professors won't bother sending their papers to minor journals, and discourage their students from doing so.

Most journals have their own submission requirements for both form and substance. Invariably, these are met with consternation by authors convinced the system is out to get them by imposing restrictive standards, such as size limitations. Most journals find it necessary to restrict the length of articles and the length of certain sections within articles. This can be very annoying to a researcher who is convinced her "groundbreaking" paper cannot possibly be shortened without losing critical substance. Complaining about "unreasonable" journal requirements and "biased" editors is a common pastime for academics the world over.

A universal criticism of this peer reviewed journal system applies to the long delays between submission and ultimate publication: a paper may undergo several revisions and take three or four years to publication. Many new forums (mostly springing up on the Internet) have begun to publish work as soon as it's received; meaning, of course, the work may not have been reviewed at all, but at least one's ideas are getting exposure, generating feedback, and helping to spur more research.

The Peer Review Process

The peer review process is a mainstay of the academic community. One's peers serve as judge and jury of one's work. Any research which has successfully passed the peer review process is formally part of the academic literature. Any work which has not been accepted by peers is deemed speculative and untested.

Peer review may be applied to selection of journal articles, speaking engagements, posters, book chapter submissions, and awards. It is also utilized in tenure decisions (discussed a bit later in this chapter).

The peer review process is typically meant to be anonymous, although the academic community within any given field may be so small and intimate that one can sometimes guess who one's reviewer was by examining the editorial feedback.

What Is a Publication?

A *publication* is an *article* or *manuscript* submitted to, and accepted by, a *journal*. The acceptance process requires reviews by one or more peers, who are generally well-established in the field. Having one's ideas and work deemed acceptable by these critics is a signal of success, as accepted articles formally join all other contributions to the field. A publication is like a stake in the ground. It's a claim on some piece of knowledge. It gives the author credit for a unique contribution. Others read the work and combine it with their own, and when they do so they're required to cite the original author(s). One measure of success for a researcher is the number of times other scientists cite his research in their papers.

Given the importance of the peer reviewed publication system, it's not surprising a fair amount of etiquette and procedure is involved. Generally, the author listed first is recognized as the most significant contributor, and receives the most prestige. In fields requiring laboratory work, anyone who is a member of the laboratory, with even a minor contribution, may be listed as an author. There can easily be eight or more authors on such articles. By convention, the leader of the laboratory may place her name as the first author, even if she hasn't done the majority of the work. Not all participants adhere to these strict conventions. In some fields, it is more typical to list authors alphabetically, although this is more common when there are just a handful of contributors.

The process of submitting an article to a journal, and having it accepted for publication, can be lengthy and frustrating. Many express concern that the process is susceptible to political manipulation. For example, a famous professor's work may be accepted without the rigorous review applied to a junior professor's submission. While this may be seen as the privilege a proven veteran deserves, it can lead to the publishing of inferior material, as even well-established researchers occasionally produce subpar material, just as famous artists occasionally produce an inferior painting.

As frustrating as the submission and review process may seem, the learning process is valuable: one should make an effort to stay cool and take the opportunity to objectively assess one's work. Is it good enough? Is it *really* good enough? Can the arguments made in the article withstand scrutiny? Are the claims made in the paper defensible? Graduate students must learn to be self-critical and accept criticism constructively, even if the delivery is somewhat offensive.

There are numerous stories of lengthy and bureaucratic submission processes. Depending on the field, a paper may undergo several revisions and resubmissions over a period of as many as three or four years. There can frequently be disagreements between the reviewer or editor and the author(s). Reviewers may demand revisions which authors find absurd and unnecessary. While it's tempting to accuse the reviewer of bias and even stupidity, misunderstandings about the work may be due to the author's failure to properly and concisely make his argument. Many revision requests are legitimate and should be followed constructively; others are more stylistic and not very critical to the content, yet others are unfair and perhaps more politically motivated than one would like to believe.

A frequent refrain by a researcher is that she cannot submit a paper to a certain journal because it refutes earlier findings by an editor of that journal. Such laments hold that the submitted work is doomed from the start because, regardless of its quality, the editor would conspire to have it suspended in academic limbo for as long as possible, denying it publication.

Good editors recognize their responsibility to science, and don't consider obstructing another's discoveries, even if they do contradict their own work. Nevertheless, the human ego does play a significant role within academia. This is a world of ideas, and one tends to be very protective of the intellectual ground one has laid claim to. It's quite baffling how tenaciously academics will argue in favor of their theories. "Academic debates are very intensely heated—because there is nothing at stake" is a very old saying; it's quite cheap to carry on an argument, verbally or in print, and one can be as defiant as a mountain. There's no pecuniary penalty; as the issues are usually quite murky, there is rarely a clear winner. What better setting to have an argument? One can get all huffy, blow off steam, tenaciously defend a position, and not have to pay any price for taking the stand.

People often think of a publication one-dimensionally—as a crucial stepping stone to tenure. The full meaning and value of a publication goes beyond tenure decisions: each publication is one building block in the grand efforts to discover the secrets of our universe. The world is full of mysteries; these abound, regardless of the field of study. No individual is capable of unlocking all the secrets of even one of these fields. Multiple researchers in each field and subfield nibble away at these hidden truths, using individual papers in an effort to slice off a piece of the great unknown and clarify it somewhat. Each researcher contributes pieces of a giant puzzle. This is why the astute researchers recognize their contribution would amount to nothing had they not been able to stand on the shoulders of others.

One of the challenges of publications is that rigid thinking or flawed research produces weak building blocks, forcing others to take a few steps backward before going forward again. Thus, the process of unveiling the mysteries of the universe is more of a drunken stagger than an orderly march. Nevertheless, it's the only system in place today.

Examples of obstacles and backward steps are early beliefs the earth was flat, or the earth was the center of the universe. Each of these beliefs was so ingrained in earlier societies that many centuries of advancement were lost. Brave researchers who sensed the errors in these theories suffered more than ridicule—they were often subjected to corporal or capital punishment. For them, the academic debate was quite dangerous: their pieces of the grand puzzle were paid for with blood. This isn't to say that today's scholars must make a comparable physical sacrifice, but it's useful to have a broader perspective when evaluating a journal reviewer's seemingly critical opinion of one's work.

What Is an Abstract?

An *abstract* is a *summary* of an academic paper or article, usually limited to a single paragraph, which succinctly explains the full article, and highlights the results or conclusions.

Abstracts play a crucial role in the academic world, supporting much-needed efficiency. There may be dozens or hundreds of articles written in a particular field in a given year or even month. No one has the time to read through each and every one of these often lengthy and dense documents. The abstract allows for quick filtration: the reader can scan the abstract, immediately get a sense of the article's content, what it claims to have discovered and contributed to the literature.

Needless to say, a poorly written abstract reflects poorly on the author, and all but guarantees the complete article will not be read. Similarly, an abstract that inaccurately portrays the article's contents is also likely to hurt the author's reputation, and reduce the likelihood that his or her contributions will be read in future. Thus, time spent on polishing and refining an abstract is well spent.

First Author

When there are multiple authors, there is extra prestige associated with being listed first in the author list. Traditionally, this listing is reserved for the most senior and famous professor, the professor leading the laboratory, or, in the most democratic cases, to the professor who actually did most of the work. Then and now, when being considered for tenure, first authorships carry more weight.

In recent years, the convention has shifted somewhat to a simple alphabetic listing, although a significant contributor may still be given special billing by being placed first on the list.

Tenure

Tenure can be thought of as a lifetime employment guarantee. It's typically awarded in recognition of significant contribution to one's field and institution. For many, obtaining tenure is the height of academic achievement, affirming one's intellect and achievements and significant job security.

The perks of tenure have always been highly sought after; Julie Lynem's comment in the *San Francisco Chronicle* a few years ago is an excellent summation:

> For aspiring university professors, tenure is supposed to be the ultimate reward. A permanent faculty appointment is perceived by many to be academic nirvana.[9]

One interpretation of tenure was humorously encapsulated by a tenured professor, who explained it thus:

> Tenure means that the only way I can be fired from my university position is if I'm caught having an affair with a married woman—whose husband is the university president. And even then I would have to be handsomely compensated on my way out!

It's important to note that members of the academic community see tenure as far more than run-of-the-mill job security. They see it as a critical mechanism preserving freedom of speech. The argument in favor of tenure is that the guarantee of employment allows academics to voice their theories and opinions without fear of repercussions from the establishment, which may otherwise fire them or threaten to do so in an effort to stifle dissent.

A tenured professor is a member of an exclusive club, with the right to vote for or against future tenure applicants. Another privilege of tenure in certain institutions is free university education for immediate family members. In some cases, there are agreements with other universities to extend this perk to a whole network of institutions.

Tenured professors may also be eligible for sabbatical periods. A sabbatical leave or year is effectively a break, during which the academic may travel, write a book, spend time in another institution, or generally undertake some activities which differ from normal day-to-day activities. Many universities allow a professor one sabbatical year for each six years of on-campus work. Often, there is at least some partial funding by one's original institution; in some cases, funding is full for the entire year. In others, the host institution, if there is one, may also provide some funding.

Tenure is generally awarded based on a candidate's performance in three areas:

1. Research and publication record
2. Teaching record
3. Evidence of service to the institution

The tenacious fight for tenure can turn quite ugly and, occasionally, petty. An assistant professor may be denied tenure on the grounds of a fourth tenure requirement—failing the collegiality test, which basically means he doesn't get along well with colleagues. Some universities shy away from including this as a criterion, as it is more likely to lead to legal action by the rejected candidate.

While a candidate for tenure should ideally meet all the above criteria, the common view is that the most essential component of one's qualification for tenure is a proven publication record. Publications lend prestige to the academic institution, and it's in the best interest of all faculty members that their tenured colleagues pull their weight in producing these publications. Publications in leading journals are especially prized and significant in one's tenure bid. Most departments provide at least implicit guidance on the number of required publications for tenure. It's best to strive to surpass these benchmarks, not just meet them.

The actual required number of publications differs across fields and universities. Often, the "required" number is never explicitly stated, to give the voting faculty more flexibility in rejecting a candidate.

The almost-exclusive emphasis on research during tenure decisions has come under great criticism, because it often comes at the expense of a candidate's teaching record. From society's perspective, a professor's teaching capability may have more impact than a publication record: many publications are read by a handful of people and do relatively little to further the cause of science. A prolific publisher who is a poor educator may be responsible for producing hundreds or thousands of poorly educated and/or demotivated people, while multiple publications rarely have such a significant impact on society. Recognizing the need for better-educated undergraduates, a number of schools have, in recent years, made (or at least claimed to make) an effort to change tenure requirements and add more weight to educational contributions. This has been (at least partly) due to heightened consumer activism by parents and students who've seen the costs of education rise, yet feel they are not getting their money's worth.

Teaching is generally a far more important component of tenure at small, liberal arts colleges that emphasize quality education. While teaching ability often takes a back seat in the tenure decision at major research universities, a department may be more inclined to offer tenure to someone who can teach the most difficult courses, or those no one else wants to teach.

Faculties hope a young professor will be motivated by the promise of tenure and work hard to attain it, in the process bringing prestige to herself and to her university. The expectation is that, once awarded tenure, the professor will continue with her commitment and diligent work habits on both the research and teaching fronts. This is the win-win situation for the aspiring academic and her Faculty. Unfortunately, upon attaining tenure some professors elect to rest on their laurels, and cut back on their efforts to publish and teach, in a sense, going against the spirit of the academic tenure arrangement. Reducing teaching and research efforts is universally frowned upon; many tenured professors are reluctant to confirm an applicant's tenure until they are convinced he will continue to contribute to research efforts, and carry an appropriate teaching load.

Failure to achieve tenure is universally seen as a slap in the face, a harsh message that one is not good enough, usually accompanied by the loss of one's job, or voluntary departure by the professor, who is inclined to seek tenure elsewhere.

The full process of obtaining tenure typically takes five or six years. The tenure clock begins to count down from the moment the assistant professor enters a tenure-track position: the candidate may begin by signing a three-year contract with the school, with the understanding that a two- or three-year extension will be offered if performance is satisfactory. There is at least one evaluation event two or three years into the tenure bid; the candidate may meet with the department chair for feedback—advice as to where and how to focus her bid for tenure. Occasionally, the applicant will be told performance to date has been poor, and encouraged to plan accordingly—that is, begin looking for a position elsewhere. The most obvious signal tenure has been denied is when one's initial contract isn't extended.

Being denied tenure is generally devastating at the time—it's an important point in one's professional life. Some people are turned down for the right reasons: they simply were not able to muster the requirements, and it's time they look elsewhere. Knowing this sooner, rather than later, is better for all concerned. Those who have the talent, but are rejected for other reasons, should find out what these reasons are. Perhaps they need only work on a few small things and become eligible. There is always the possibility of obtaining tenure at another university. Often, once turned down by a very good school, a professor may be welcomed by a school where he is a better "fit." The key is to use the rejection constructively. If you find yourself in this position, rather than holding a grudge, motivate yourself to be better. Some day your achievements may make the rejecting institution regret their decision.

It's quite possible to be a late bloomer for tenure qualification: not everyone can be ready for the tenure verdict on the same schedule. An obvious and legitimate reason for missing a tenure decision deadline is family obligation: many young professors place their tenure race ahead of all other priorities; others choose family first—a perfectly legitimate decision which may slow academic progress.

Some candidates find themselves in the enviable position of having their tenure decision accelerated, in cases where the applicant's performance has been outstanding, and/or when the standing tenured faculty has shrunk. Shrinkage is typically due to attrition—retirements or departures of veteran faculty, leaving a void which must be filled quickly; the faculty may vote on tenure a year or two early. When faced with a highly talented candidate, the faculty has the incentive to vote early as untenured but outstanding candidates may be wooed by other universities.

Tenure is usually formally awarded following a vote by the tenured professors within a department (e.g., the biology department). Sometimes, the vote may be necessary but not sufficient; approval at the Faculty level (once the professors in the biology department approve a candidate, the Life Sciences Faculty might also have a say) may be required. Ratification by a university body such as the university senate may be required in some institutions. Sometimes good candidates, acceptable to their department, may not receive tenure due to a veto from a higher level in the bureaucratic pyramid for budgetary reasons, political machinations, or poor marketing of the applicant.

Some of the more common reasons for denial of tenure are:

- Inadequate research record. The most common deficiency is that an academic's publication record is considered weak by the standing faculty. It's noteworthy that strength of publication record is a relative thing. The best programs may require a half-dozen publications in the best journals. Less-prestigious schools may accept the same number of publications in lesser journals, while the least competitive programs may accept just two or three publications in any journal.

- Inadequate teaching record. Tenure may be denied when an instructor consistently receives very low ratings, and/or is the subject of frequent complaints by students. While a university focused on research may overlook a brilliant researcher's poor teaching performance, a small liberal arts college which emphasizes quality education will act decisively and deny tenure.

- Lack of service to the institution. A professor is required to contribute to the institution in a number of ways, including serving on various committees, acting as liaison with other departments, and traveling to represent the institution at conferences or recruiting functions. Failure to do one's share may be grounds for denial of tenure.

- Political machination within the department. One may be rejected for various political reasons; there may be several cliques within the department, and the clique the assistant professor belongs to may not be powerful enough to push through his application. The cliques may be vying for a limited funding pool or number of hiring slots and may see the awarding of tenure to an outsider as being at the expense of their group's access to funds or future like-minded colleagues. While hardly satisfying, at least in this case one can take comfort in knowing that one's performance has been good, and it should be possible to find tenure elsewhere.

- Personal animosity. For a real or imagined reason, an assistant professor may have alienated one or more senior faculty members who speak forcefully against him during the voting session. It's very difficult to recover from a focused attack by a senior faculty member. The only hope in these situations is that a more powerful member of the faculty takes it upon herself to defend the candidate.

Lifetime employment guarantees are expensive: granting tenure has become less frequent at many schools. Some have even abolished the concept and no longer offer the traditional package. Instead, schools have gravitated to increased reliance on nontenured faculty with fewer benefits. Some argue this has created two tiers of academics: those with tenure and full benefits, versus those who have few to no benefits and are effectively treated as second-class citizens.

There is one achievement which is even better than obtaining tenure: a chair or chairmanship. A chair is typically funded by a philanthropist or corporation, and provides some stipend as well as prestige to the endowed professor. The stipend may be used to fortify the professor's salary and/or support her research efforts. Chairs are often bestowed for the balance of a professor's career.

Receiving a prestigious chair is equivalent to being voted to an all-star team. Extending the analogy, receiving a Nobel prize is equivalent to being voted to the hall of fame of academics.

Why God Never Received Tenure

> *He had only one major publication which had no references and was never in a refereed journal. The scientific community has found it impossible to replicate his results. As for his teaching skills: His office hours were infrequent and usually held on a mountaintop, and rather than coming to class he simply insisted that students just read his Book. Worse still, he expelled his first two students for learning.* -Anonymous

Academic Conferences

Ideas are among the most important intellectual commodities: they take on greater value when shared with others. Prior to the communication options afforded by technological innovations such as the Internet, the most effective way for professors to reach beyond the borders of their own university and their relatively limited cadre of colleagues was through conferences. While technology now makes it much easier to communicate and collaborate, conferences remain a mainstay of academic life. They typically occur annually, attract a critical mass of interested parties in a particular field, and are used for information exchange. They are also useful venues for presenting one's work to an interested and critical audience.

Conferences also provide a meeting place to explore employment opportunities, and very importantly, as a setting for pursuing social ties to rarely seen colleagues and friends. Many academic organizations arrange these get-togethers in appealing locations to atone for the relative lack of perks. Many participants, especially more senior and established academics, bring their spouses as well. Depending on the particular field, conferences may attract business and political leaders in addition to members of the academic community.

As academic fields have grown, conferences have become highly specialized. For example, today there may be separate conferences catering to academics in the fields of banking, financial risk management, and investment management. Thirty years ago, these individuals may have all congregated at just one general economics conference. Similar growth and specialization has affected all other academic fields; conferences are far more numerous, and many have grown significantly in size. The largest may attract thousands of participants, and have become so logistically challenging small cities can no longer accommodate them.

Often, corporations (large and small) serve as conference sponsors. This can be a double-edged sword for academic purists: corporate sponsorship money can reduce conference fees for attendees, may allow for venue upgrades, and generally help put on a better event. However, accepting money from for-profit organizations can create the impression, if not the reality, that the academic process is influenced by industry motives and biases.

With the dawn of the technological age, one may have hypothesized that conference participation would become less important; interestingly, these congregations remain very popular, partly because the prestige associated with presenting at such events has increased over time. Some conferences attract keynote addresses by Nobel laureates, high-ranking government officials, and icons of business communities, giving attendees an opportunity to rub elbows with academic and non-academic celebrities.

Some academic conferences are better organized and attended than others; some attract a thin audience or poor speakers, others fail logistically. Young researchers may purposely arrange for speaking engagements in the smaller, less-prestigious venues with a view to "cutting their teeth" in a less-intimidating environment. As their confidence and public speaking skills improve, they are more comfortable setting their sights higher.

Some students feel it's their duty to go to conferences, but once they arrive, they don't participate in anything. There are no points for just showing up! The key is to make good use of one's time and opportunities, especially when affordability constraints mean students typically attend a very small number of conferences a year. The wise ones make the most of the experience, attending as many talks as possible, reading posters, making small talk with others, listening carefully to their opinions, collecting and handing out business cards to establish lines of communication, and sharing thoughts about mutual research interests. Nurtured contacts can lead to future research collaborations, even job offers.

Understandably, it is often less intimidating for students to speak with junior professors and graduate students than Nobel laureates. Beginning with "entry-level" colleagues is an excellent career move, because a peer group advances in knowledge and seniority. Over time, these relationships may blossom into deep friendships and professional collaborations, and the entire cohort becomes "The Establishment," with its share of stars and heavy hitters.

Attending a conference is useful for all the reasons recounted above, but there are more meaningful, *Curriculum Vitae*-building activities:

- Speaking engagements
- Keynote addresses
- Panel discussions
- Poster presentations

Speaking Engagement

A conference speaking engagement is a formal presentation by one or several presenters. These are arranged well in advance and are often awarded after a peer review process in which a committee considers a number of potential speakers on various topics and selects the subset which reflects (in the committee's opinion) the most important research, of most relevance to the expected audience. It should be assumed that these sessions are formal. Conference speakers are often identifiable by a ribbon on their conference identification badge, which may also bear the legend "Speaker." A perk associated with speaking engagements is that the speaker is often not required to pay the conference registration fee, which may range from a few hundred to a few thousand dollars. Speaking engagements are important entries on a *Curriculum Vitae*.

Furthermore, following a conference presentation, the presenter may be approached with other invitations to present on a similar topic at a university, institute, government, or corporate event. Often, the institution extending the invitation will pay the presenter's expenses and may also provide an honorarium (small sum of money).

While a speaking engagement is prestigious in its own right, the ultimate engagement is a keynote address.

Keynote Address

A keynote address is a speaking engagement, but far more prestigious in that it is either the only, or one of a small number of, featured presentations in a large conference. While a conference may have dozens or hundreds of speaking slots, often run in several parallel (simultaneous) streams, the keynote address(es) are designed to attract maximum attendance, as plenary (or full) sessions.

The keynote speaker may be further distinguished from run-of-the-mill speakers by a distinctly colored ribbon and the sought-after legend, "Keynote Speaker." Often, these speakers (or single speaker) will be singled out for special perks such as dinner invitations, fancy accommodations, and, in some cases, financial compensation. They are often also included by conference organizers as panelists in panel discussions. Such participation is often seen as a way to get the most value out of a distinguished (and expensive) guest. Keynote addresses are highly prestigious examples of an academic's standing among her peers, and are highly prized *CV* entries.

Panel Discussion

A panel discussion, as the name implies, usually brings together a number (typically three to five) of experts, who weigh in on a particular subject. Such sessions are occasionally referred to as roundtables. Often, a moderator will be assigned to each session and will begin by soliciting responses to several key questions from the panelists. In some cases, the microphone or floor is subsequently opened to the audience who may direct questions to the panel as a whole or to individual panelists. Participation as panelist and/or moderator should be included in one's *CV*.

Poster Presentation

An explicit purpose of conferences is to allow participants access to others' work. The information exchange is considered a primary function of such events. In addition to formal public sessions (presentations and panels), poster presentations are available as a way to advertise and share one's work. In a poster presentation, the presenter creates a large poster, often on the order of 24 by 36 inches (60 by 90 cm). The poster contains a prominent, and, one hopes, catchy title, as well as brief descriptions of findings and methodology. Posters are displayed in halls, usually lined up in rows, allowing room for viewers to walk along, scanning titles. While on display, each poster must be accompanied by at least one presenter, who is available to answer the questions of passers-by. A poster is usually displayed for two or three hours. It is then removed and replaced by another team's poster. Posters are often grouped by theme, maximizing the benefit for viewers who have a particular interest in that area of study, as they can spend a few hours catching up quickly on a broad swath of work in progress. Even a small conference can be a venue for hundreds of poster presentations.

Posters are often not published work. In some cases there is a superficial peer review process for accepting posters to a conference. While far less prestigious than a speaking engagement or panel session, a poster presentation is a legitimate form of participation in the academic process. It should be listed on one's *CV*.

Competition for Scarce Resources

Almost universally, three resources are scarce on any university campus: most obvious is funding, followed by human resources, and space. Predictably, resource shortages are accompanied by stress, bickering, complaints, and/or pitched battles.

Scarcity is, of course, relative. The most prominent private institutions—the Ivy League schools, Stanford and Massachusetts Institute of Technology (MIT), etc.—have multibillion dollar endowments, enabling them to build modern facilities and attract prominent professors, who, in turn, attract more funding and high quality students. Active fund-raising efforts and advanced alumni networks ensure a healthy flow of funds to these institutions. Some of these wealthy universities may be space-constrained, but their access to financial resources lessens the pain considerably. Thus, on average, professors and students at these more privileged schools are subject to fewer resource constraints than those in most other institutions.

Funding Shortages

Funding shortages affect some Faculties and departments more than others.

The arts, and more generally the humanities, are often hard-pressed for funding, while business schools, medical schools, life sciences programs, and some engineering programs have far more funding available. The simple explanation for this is that academic findings in engineering, biotech, business, and medicine have immediate commercial applications. High profile academic advances can readily lead to huge financial windfalls, attracting funding from corporations and governments. In contrast, wherever there is little commercial interest, the major source of funding is often from government sources. Inevitably, as governments at all levels struggle with budget constraints, funding for research and education suffer.

Another factor affecting the relative availability of funds is resource intensity of the research in question. Some research is naturally more expensive than others; applied physics and biology, for example, may require expensive laboratory setups and materials. Without significant funds, much of the work would grind to a halt. In contrast, theoretical explorations in physics, mathematics, or economics may require little more than a run-of-the-mill desktop computer.

Human Resource Constraints

An obvious constraint in a given department is too few professors to teach coursework, leading to larger classes, and higher student-to-professor ratios, which may lead to hiring more adjunct professors to cover teaching responsibilities. As a result, professors may have to teach more classes and have less time for research.

Academic human resource constraints are often addressed by using graduate students to help with teaching and research. Professors need graduate students' help with their more tedious chores, and are happy to secure such services at a fraction of the cost of their own time. Students who can capably help in teaching or research allow a professor to leverage his time and publish more. Given the importance of publications, the competition for the most talented students can be quite intense.

Space Limitations

The final frontier of resource scarcity is space. Not the kind strewn with galaxies and individual stars, but the one where laboratories and offices are located. Institutions experience natural growth: they expand, and facilities must expand in step. Universities usually attempt to squeeze more employees and facilities into existing buildings, significantly affecting the quality of life for all concerned. The direct cost of this crowding is some faculty and administrators may elect to go elsewhere. Eventually, to remain competitive, all universities must commit to large-scale construction projects, and are, invariably, forced to deal with internal bickering and maneuvering as the various Faculties and departments fight to secure the new space.

Despite the recent decline in property values, it isn't trivial to add space without incurring high costs. Urban universities face the highest constraints, with real physical limitations on expansion.

The Less-Collegial College

There are many who think of the academic world as idyllic, unspoiled by egos, politics, or conflict—an unfortunately naïve view. Academic institutions are rife with politics and overinflated egos. Some of the conflicts inherent to academic institutions are listed below.

Clash of Egos

Scholars have spent millennia trying to prove they are smarter than one another. Heated competition can positively drive research, discovery, and innovation; however, competition can lead to distraction and destruction.

The absurdity such clashes can lead to is embodied in this true story, involving two professors at a highly respected university. Each felt he was the most accomplished in the department. Rather than collaborate to establish an even greater whole, the two were always at each other's throats. The rivalry came to a head when Professor 1 discovered that Professor 2 had a larger office. Apparently, in originally agreeing to join the university, Professor 1 had insisted upon, and been assured, he would be given the largest office in the department. The "outrage" was confirmed when Professor 1 entered Professor 2's office and proceeded to collect "evidence," using a tape measure. Indeed, one wall was six inches longer! Professor 1 promptly demanded an office swap. After much wrangling, which required intervention by several deans, a "compromise" was reached: Professor 2 would not be required to move. Instead, one wall in Professor 1's office would be moved out by 7 inches.

Repression of Competing Theories

Frequently, academics sharing a similar world-view congregate in universities where they can collaborate and support each other's efforts. Decisions to hire and offer tenure are often shaped by these core groups of like-minded researchers, ensuring their particular school of thought is propagated. An advantage to such concentrations is that researchers can collaborate intensely on one area of focus and make significant progress. A disadvantage is that this can also lead to narrow-mindedness, and repression of competing theories.

Some theory-based conflicts are fueled by more than academic dogma. An academic may view victory in the battle of ideas as a mechanism for securing prestige and an honored place in society. Often, seminal theories are inextricably linked with those who first postulated them (in some cases the theory bears the person's name). Evidence calling into question a theory's validity may tarnish not only the theory, but anyone associated with putting it forward. Thus, there is an incentive for academics to defend their ideas relentlessly for personal reasons, having nothing to do with academic precision.

And, of course, whether it's the overt physical world of flora and fauna, the micro view of molecules and subatomic particles, the cosmic heavens, or unearthing truths about social and emotional realities, academics are often called upon to support political agendas. Such partisanship can also degenerate into extremism.

A fundamentalist adherence to just one view of the world, excluding all others, leads to poorly developed scholars who, in turn, tend to dogmatically engage others in the field. Dogma—asserting an opinion as truth—is especially common when religion or nationalism is involved. Blind refusal to consider other interpretations can be dangerous for society as a whole because scientific advances are stifled; but, the danger also applies on a very personal level for scholars who find themselves in the minority school of thought.

A good example is the story of Galileo Galilei, who championed his heliocentric view of the world. Galileo believed the earth revolved around the sun, in stark contrast to the incumbent view that earth was the center of the universe; therefore, the sun revolved around the earth.

The establishment denounced Galileo as a heretic, and engaged in intimidation which eventually led to his publicly disavowing his claims. Years later, of course, it became clear Galileo's view of the world was correct.

New PhDs are well-advised to know ahead of time whether or not their ideas as students or faculty members will be well-received in certain institutions. Similarly, visiting presenters should strive to know where they'll be accepted warmly and where the audience will tear their ideas and reputations apart.

"Borrowing" Others' Ideas

Not surprisingly, the significant differences between obtaining and failing to obtain tenure have led many to behave in a less-than-stellar way. The pressure to "beat the tenure clock" has divided families, soured friendships, led to heated rivalries, and in extreme cases, to immoral or illegal behavior. The most extreme cases involve academicians who are dishonest: the key to tenure is in one's publication record; a key to a successful publication record (in addition to talent) is a deep well of research ideas which can be converted into research projects, and, ultimately, published articles. The problem with ideas is that they can be "borrowed" by others. One of the most common forms of academic dishonesty is theft of another's ideas.

Here is one example: a political scientist submits a research plan to a well-known research institute and is turned down. A year later he receives a mass email from the research center, indicating its plan to embark on a project—his original idea! He grumbles that "the academic world is one big whorehouse." This example is timeless, having been repeated in one form or another over the centuries.

Ugly Ducklings

Wherever there is a dominant school of thought, there are often smaller groups of "ugly ducklings," treated as second-class citizens; these are scholars who happen to not adhere very strongly to the more dominant school of thought present in a particular department. Alternatively, they may have no opinion at all on that particular subject, and focus on a different subfield of research. Being in the minority, however, means they will typically receive less funding; chances are, new professors interested in their chosen (minority) specialty may be hard to hire. The hiring difficulties may come in two forms: one, the candidates may be intimidated by the dominant clique and see the situation as unhealthy for their careers; two, the dominant clique will vote against hiring the candidates.

Decisions to purchase research equipment or data are often carried by the majority vote, directing the department's limited resources to its dominant factions, leaving the ugly ducklings empty-handed.

Paraphrasing Kermit the Frog, it's not easy being interested in green, when the majority is only interested in blue or red.

Romance and Sex on Campus

Stories of romance and sexual activity on college campuses are ubiquitous, occasionally the stuff of legends; but these are almost exclusively stories attributed to hormone-crazed members of the undergraduate student body.

It's often assumed that academics, including graduate students, are too overwhelmed by their workload, and are, in any event, too nerdy or socially inept to participate in romantic pursuits. In fact, professors can teach the undergraduates a thing or two about uninhibited behavior. One need not go far to come across stories of professors engaging in group sex, swapping spouses or using their offices for early afternoon conjugal adventures.

While it's easy to find juicy stories, it is nevertheless true that relationships can be difficult to maintain, especially for graduate students, often due to extreme stress. The PhD experience is all-encompassing, leaving little attention—or emotion—span for anything else. This is not to say that constructive, long-lasting relationships are impossible, but they are typically difficult.

Many relationships don't survive the graduate program, including a relatively high number of engagements and marriages. The spouse may resent the student's priorities, while the student may counter by suggesting a lack of commitment by the spouse.

Seasoned academics, while no longer concerned with the ticking of the tenure clock, face their own challenges. Many are so swept up in their fields of study their frustrated spouses describe them as "married to their work."

Relationships can be easier when both parties are students, because they can more readily relate to each other's preoccupations, moods, and stresses. Those relationships that do last through graduation inevitably reach a big hurdle as both parties seek employment; it's difficult enough to obtain *one* good academic position. Expecting to obtain two in reasonable proximity is often a tall order.

Out-of-Bounds Fraternization

While there are certainly opportunities for romance in the ivory tower, one form is prohibited on most college campuses—professors mixing with students.

Because of the obvious power a professor has over a student, such power should never be abused. Some students claim they are comfortable enough and mature enough to deal constructively with such relationships to waive any restrictions and accept responsibility. Nevertheless, the safest way to ensure that the power imbalance isn't tested is by avoiding the fraternization completely.

Many institutions have strict nonfraternization rules, essentially forbidding any professor or instructor to have any romantic interaction with a student. Sometimes, the restriction only applies to students within the professor's department or Faculty. The logic invoked in such cases is that a professor cannot influence anything that occurs in a different Faculty, and, therefore, in such situations there is no power imbalance.

Drawing a clear line demarcating acceptable and unacceptable behavior is important to the security of all concerned. It's unacceptable for students to find themselves in an imbalanced relationship with a professor. It's also important for professors to be separated from manipulation by students, who may offer sex in an effort to influence the treatment they receive at the hands of a professor. Although generally scarce, this does happen. The best defense is to always err on the side of conservatism, by avoiding compromising situations altogether.

The Academic as Stereotype

The stereotypical professor is epitomized for many by the image of Albert Einstein. The mere mention of his name immediately conjures up the kindly, slight old man with wild hair and a twinkle in his eye, standing next to a blackboard covered with mostly incomprehensible algebraic expressions. Add an outrageously outdated bowtie, a jacket with worn-out elbow patches, chronic absent-mindedness, and antisocial behavior and you've got the complete picture. Thanks to the movie *A Beautiful Mind* (2001), the stereotype of eccentricity has taken on even greater weight. The movie documents the adult life of John Nash, distinguished for his seminal work on a field which later became known as game theory, and his eccentric behavior, which was attributed to schizophrenia.

Further propagating the eccentric stereotype are those professors who delight in getting students' attention by climbing on top of their desks, singing in class, reciting rhyming poems written for students' birthdays, complaining that recent Nobel prize recipients stole their work, and even those who are so gullible they buy elevator passes from students, only to discover there are no elevators on campus.

The "academic" traits of disconnected, absent-minded, antisocial behavior are almost exclusively associated with male faculty. Readers of John Gray's *Men are from Mars, Women are from Venus* may recognize some of this behavior as being consistent with the male's need, on occasion, to go into his "cave." In recent decades, more women have joined the professorial ranks, and established that they can be as absent-minded a group of cave dwellers as their male counterparts.

Academics frequently shut out the rest of the world, go into their intellectual caves where they can introspect, examine a problem without interruptions or interference, and eventually come out when the problem is solved. Eating, sleeping, and interacting with others become secondary during this hibernation. Most academics need not make use of a physical cave (or office); it's quite possible to enter this cave intellectually and remain in it while wandering aimlessly across campus. Most behavior perceived by the world at large as eccentric is merely a result of this highly focused state, during which academics are completely preoccupied with their thoughts.

The antisocial or curmudgeon characterization may have its roots in the fact that the academic community can be the ultimate IQ-haven (for high-powered analytical minds), at the expense of emotional competence (or people skills). As the old joke goes, the academic community ends up becoming home to the misfits who can't hold down a real-world job.

Church and Mortarboard

"Your Highness, I have no need of this hypothesis." - Pierre Laplace (1749-1827), to Napoleon on why his works on celestial mechanics make no mention of God.

There have been, of course, momentous conflicts between secular scholarship and religion. One need not go back too many years in Europe to find bitter persecution of scientists and scholars whose scientific discoveries were at odds with traditional religious doctrine. Since those dark ages, scholars in traditionally closed religious societies have made important gains. Many of these gains must be attributed to courageous efforts of individuals, while some of the credit belongs with the broader global academic community, which has been able to impose its collective weight. The battle for freedom of opinion and freedom of speech is far from won, however. To this day, there are religious bodies which refuse to accept or teach evolutionary theories. There are religious councils which impose death sentences on scholars whose literature is deemed blasphemous; these religious councils' day-to-day sermons preach in favor of insularity and closed-mindedness, and against enlightenment and tolerance.

Even in the more "enlightened" democracies, the battle for separation of church and education is ongoing. Stories abound of parents strong-arming school districts into continuing to give the theory of creation or "intelligent design" equal (or more) time than evolution theories; there are ongoing cases of teachers imposing religious standards or rites on students. These are usually overturned by the legal system once brought into the public eye. Legal challenges revolving around religious issues are frequently made against universities by individuals, clubs, and fraternities.

While the academic community has traditionally been a champion of freedom and tolerance, and a bulwark against extremism, academic institutions are sometimes guilty of intolerance and incitement to violence. This phenomenon has most recently been seen in a number of countries in the Middle East and Southeast Asia, where institutions of higher learning sponsor fundamentalist viewpoints and incite against liberalism and open-mindedness.

Ethics

"Copy from one, it's plagiarism; copy from two, it's research." - Wilson Mizner (1876-1933)

Many people consider the possibility of dishonesty in the ivory tower unthinkable. Yet, in reality, fear, ego, and competition have contributed to lapses on the part of students and faculty members. Members of both communities may succumb to fear about their careers and future prospects, leading them to cheat or tinker with results. Egos and competition have led to similar impulses.

Student Cheating

Many students find the prospect of obtaining a university education, especially at a well-regarded school, critical to their success in life. The pressure to gain entry into such institutions and succeed in them is intense. This leads to healthy competition, but also has its downside in unhealthy, or dishonest, competition. The pressure on students can begin very early, convincing them they must succeed in a long sequence of events beginning in high school. Such pressure may come from a need to please one's parents, or a response to peer pressure.

The pressure to get into the "right" school has led to several forms of misrepresentation by students. A *USA Today* article[10] explores increasing concerns that students are lying on their applications. The article makes it clear the number of students actually doctoring résumés is small, but the practice does appear to be on the rise. Résumés sent to university admissions offices abound with claims of captaincies of teams, presidencies of clubs, and a plethora of valedictorians (graduates with the highest grade point average). There isn't anything surprising about applicants to outstanding schools having such distinctions on their résumés. The issue is increasingly with having multiple students claiming to have achieved these from the same school! In other words, students these days all seem to be "above average."

High competition at the nation's leading institutions, one may argue, pressures students to cut corners. Leading schools may appear, on occasion, to underreport such activities, out of fear that accurate reporting would hurt the school's image and damage its standing. Students caught red-handed are frequently let off rather easily, with a symbolic slap on the wrist.

There is an understandable fear that students who get away with cheating at school are more likely to exhibit integrity deficiencies once they leave school for employment. The media continually reports stories of high-level corporate corruption, insider trading, conspiracies, and obstruction of justice. Should the academic community shoulder the blame for ethical lapses within the business community? The Enron and WorldCom debacles (among others) caused the nation's business schools to revisit the ethics components of their curricula. The *Financial Times*[11] reports many business schools, such as Harvard's, are now making ethics a required course. It's noteworthy that such moves are not unanimously applauded; some administrators don't feel ethics should be compulsory within an already overstretched business program, and view the matter of ethics as a personal issue between a person and his or her moral standards, which are not a university's responsibility.

Faculty Cheating

Faculty members also have skeletons in their ethics closets. A *Scientific American* article discusses two physicists from Bell Laboratories and Lawrence Berkeley National Laboratory who were fired for allegedly manipulating results.[12] While many within the academic community hesitate to pass judgment, the author reports, "some regard these episodes as a wake-up call for a field that has considered fraud within its ranks a freak occurrence." Concerns about an increase in fraudulent results have lent some momentum to efforts within science journals and academic departments to be more vigilant.

In addition to matters of fraud such as those recounted above, faculty members occasionally run afoul of patent and intellectual rights laws; these infringement battles may be fought between academics and corporations they work with, or between professors and their universities. The issues often hinge on who retains the rights for inventions, patents, and other intellectual property produced by faculty while working in corporate or university facilities.

Questionable behavior isn't limited to students and faculty: an Associated Press article in *The Australian*[13] reports that administrators are not exempt, recounting how admissions officials at Princeton hacked into Yale's admissions notification web site. These two venerable institutions have a long history of trying to best each other in admitting the best students. Even allowing for some tradition of competition, such behavior, if true, crosses a red line.

Brain Drain

Brain drain, the migration of talent from one entity or location to another, is a concern for many countries around the world. American universities have historically been the main beneficiaries of much of this outflow from other countries; the issue traditionally hasn't been problematic from America's point of view. Following the attacks of September 11, 2001, greater difficulty in renewing or obtaining visas has created some concerns that productive students and professors will be less likely to apply to, or remain in, the United States.

Brain drain is a highly contentious issue in many countries, including, for example, Canada and Australia. Hundreds of thousands of their talented medical practitioners, business people, artists, and scientists in all fields enrich America's stores of human capital at the expense of their home countries' intellectual wealth. The best solution is to make similar career options for these people available in their home countries—the solution, therefore, lies mostly within those countries. The United States has attempted to help by providing temporary visas requiring graduates to return to their home countries where their enhanced talent may be of benefit. Nevertheless, many of these people wait a few years and attempt, once again, to move to the USA.

Some nations, recognizing the potential damage to their own academic institutions and commerce, are taking action to stem the outward flow of talent. Australia began awarding Federation Fellowships to promising academics to keep its intellectual "athletes" at home.[14]

Within the United States, there is also a growing migration of the best professors from land grant and other state-supported universities and teachers colleges to the Ivy League and other wealthy institutions. With burgeoning endowments, modern facilities, and associated prestige, the latter are able to hire up-and-coming stars from less wealthy schools. As the endowment gap grows, it becomes harder and harder for the public and less wealthy private institutions to compete and keep their most productive scholars. This escalating migration pattern has been the subject of much attention in recent years, as concern grows that a small number of universities is hoarding all the talent.

There is another very common brain drain: academics leave the academic community and join the world of business. Given the very insular view academics often take of their precious ivory tower, those who depart for the corporate world are often seen as selling out the principles and purity of academe.

The "sold out" tag may also be applied to a professor who, rather than physically depart for greener corporate pastures, has nominally remained a faculty member, but begun to cater to popular interests.

This "prostitution"—selling out the purity of scholarship for something as crass as money—is necessarily the sole purview of a tenured academic. A junior (nontenured) professor could never hope to survive and be given tenure if he or she exhibits any "love of the masses," or connection to any other world outside academe.

Some of the enmity directed at academic prostitutes is fair, but some of it is not. Criticizing academicians legitimately providing a service or product to a broad audience is not altogether fair; the offering may not be rigorous by strict academic standards, but may still provide fair value to its recipients. An example would be an economics or finance professor writing a practitioner-oriented book about investment management. However, if the prostitute has sold out the rigors of academic principles and is taking advantage of populist products, catering to the masses in cheap, possibly misleading ways, he is fairly criticized. An example would be a medical researcher who supports a dubious hair replacement product or markets unnecessary and potentially dangerous cosmetic surgery services.

Jealousy is typically the emotion underlying criticism of professors who take advantage of external opportunities. It may be easier to understand such emotional responses by considering the following: scholars spend their entire lives undertaking what each considers earth-shattering research. They toil for years to become editors of the most prestigious journals in their field (readership: 16 people). When all is said and done, they have a barely adequate pension. This makes it difficult to cheer on the successes of a former colleague who is parading around in the latest sports car and talking about her new yacht.

Chapter 11: Hot Issues in the Academic World

The rigors of a graduate program often completely absorb students, to the exclusion of all other considerations. Because of this preoccupation, some students fail to notice major issues the academic community is struggling with. Post graduation, new PhDs suddenly find themselves immersed in the realities of their academic communities. Some of these realities include the following issues:

- Failures in higher education
- Innovation in education
- Money matters
- Affirmative action and diversity
- Tenure erosion and part-time professorships
- Grade inflation
- Intellectual property rights

Interestingly, the most important of these have been critical issues for the academic community over many centuries.

Failure in Higher Education

Educating others is far more than *verbatim* recital of text book content: teaching requires making a connection, recognizing that not every student understands a concept the first time, realizing that if the audience doesn't get it, the answer isn't to dismiss them as stupid, but to look within first and ask, "Have I failed to explain this properly?"

Intellectual centers, such as universities, are surely among mankind's most impressive creations; however, only a narrow-minded fool would mistake the ivory tower for a perfect educational setting. Some deficiencies in our current system may be identified by asking and exploring the following questions:

- Is the traditional teaching model successful?
- Are today's professors qualified to teach?
- Is quantity better than quality?
- Is poor administration affecting the quality of education?

Every member of society benefits, directly and indirectly, from higher education; being well-informed, identifying those aspects of higher education which are lacking, and working toward constructive change is everyone's responsibility.

Is the Traditional Teaching Model Successful?

Are teaching techniques employed in universities today as good as they can be? Are undergraduate and graduate students properly educated? Is the academic model doing a good enough job transferring the necessary knowledge to undergraduate and graduate students? Is the appearance of alternatives to traditional schools (virtual programs, corporate programs) proof that the current model is failing?

Our current teaching model is not, for the most part, satisfactory; the appearance of alternatives to traditional teaching does indicate changes are needed.

Thomas H. Benton explores some of these questions in a pair of *Chronicle of Higher Education* articles. He initially focuses on the failings of students in institutions of higher education.[15] His aptly titled piece, "The 7 Deadly Sins of Students," includes the following:

> Enabled by institutions, students repeatedly take the path of least resistance, imagining they are making creative compromises with duty that express their unique talents. So they choose self-indulgence instead of self-denial and self-esteem instead of self-questioning. They do not understand that those choices will eventually cause more unhappiness than the more difficult paths they chose not to walk.

Benton then turns the argument around with a subsequent article, "The 7 Deadly Sins of Professors." [16] The article includes the observations from a professor's perspective:

> We cultivate students' unmerited pride with high praise for mediocre work. And we tolerate all of the other sins by abdicating responsibility for the culture of our classrooms. Again and again, I have heard students say their classes are so easy that almost no effort is required, even for top grades. Residential student life, at many institutions, is mostly free time to explore and indulge one's vices. And we professors—too busy chasing our ambitions—avoid maintaining standards because they are time-consuming and costly to our teaching evaluations.

One could argue endlessly whether blame for the failings of the current higher education system are due to students or their instructors—the likely truth is both parties share blame. However, ultimate responsibility rests with the academic community to dictate and enforce effective teaching methods that ensure students have sufficient structure to avoid self-indulgence. Research exploring how we learn, and under which circumstances we learn best, is currently underway: the academic community must make consistent, conscious efforts to find and embrace new techniques to transfer knowledge.

Are Today's Professors Qualified to Teach?

A strong argument can be made that the answer to this question is No!

Kindergarten, elementary and high school teachers are required to study *how to teach*, and must proceed through a fairly regimented system to attain the appropriate credentials. PhDs, responsible for teaching at the highest levels of higher education, traditionally have very little to no formal training in how to teach, instruct, train, or educate others. It's assumed that, somehow, students obtain their PhDs and simultaneously (and miraculously) acquire the ability to teach, perhaps by osmosis. They are subsequently entrusted with educating our most advanced students: the next generation of leaders, thinkers, poets, scientists, philosophers, and generals is in their hands; yet, in contrast to teaching qualifications required of elementary and secondary school teachers, university professors are required to possess few to none.

It's easy to point to the global dominance of North American-educated leaders and insist that the system is, nevertheless, working. But where would our society be if university teachers were even better? How much *more* impact would better-educated people make on the current and future states of the world? Has the educational benefit of institutions of higher learning been maximized?

Some universities now require all graduate students to attend at least one teaching class; recently, requirements that all instructors possess at least minimal English language skills have been adopted in most North American universities. Many of these changes have come in response to complaints by irate students who felt their tuition money was wasted on graduate students and professors who were incapable of teaching, due to lack of either language or teaching skills or both. Sadly, in many cases the changes are rather cosmetic, doing relatively little to improve the quality of higher education.

In addition to poor teaching or language skills, many academics are so isolated in their ivory tower they're out of touch with external realities. Consider the examples set by many of the leading business schools: junior professors, with no practical experience outside academia, stand up in front of MBA students and preach theories. Fine, time-honored theories which make a lot of sense within the protected confines of the ivory tower, but are difficult or impossible to apply in the complex global marketplace that is today's real business environment. It doesn't take long for an MBA student with up to ten years of work experience to challenge the professor's statements; the inadequately prepared professor cannot bridge this gap between theory and practice for the confused students. As a result, some of the material is rendered useless, and the instructor's credibility is eroded.

Is Quantity Better than Quality?

Have schools become assembly lines, efficiently producing large numbers of graduates, who have lower-quality educations?

In some ways, the institution of higher education has become too much of a business: the American system of higher education is a net exporter to the tune of billions of dollars annually. Thousands of foreign students consume American education each year; this, in itself, should not be an issue: it is, in fact, on the face of it, reason to celebrate. It is a privilege to have knowledge which can be shared with others. Rather, the problem is that as American education has become more of an industry, it has also developed some of the traits shared by other mature industries, namely mechanized production. In our context, the "product" of these factories is the university graduate, fresh off the college assembly line. The output of these gigantic factories includes hundreds of thousands of professional school graduates in the fields of engineering, business, nursing, law, and medicine, and thousands of PhDs in all these fields, and many others, as well. While assembly lines can be efficient in the sense of cost, when dealing with human beings there is always a price in terms of humanity and individuality. Less faculty time spent one-on-one with students, along with other resource constraints, lead to lower-quality output.

Is Poor Administration Affecting the Quality of Education?

Another issue in academia is the quality of administrative functions within institutions of higher learning. Some administrators are truly professionals; however, many are poor managers. The latter may embark on wasteful pet projects, block necessary initiatives aimed at increasing efficiency, alienate employees leading to departures of key personnel, etc. Bad managers drain resources that should be applied to improving education quality. Professors who turn to administrative roles may also neglect their remaining teaching duties, creating another, perhaps less obvious, negative effect on education quality, as they no longer care about teaching, and may only participate to fulfill tenure or other requirements.

Wasteful, poor quality administration and lackluster teaching combine to reduce the value that academic departments are able to give back to society: poor administration saps efficiency across the board, affecting research, and slowing the pace of scientific progress.

Innovation in Education

While certain aspects of education are clearly and deservedly under fire, some innovations show promise for the future. Any aspiring or current academic should be aware of these:

- Innovative collaborations and alliances
- Creation of internal corporate education centers
- E-learning, technology, and the demise of the traditional classroom

Each of these is explored in greater detail below.

Innovative Collaborations and Alliances

Many institutions of higher learning have pooled their resources through global alliances to reach more students and to empower education and research. The architects of these joint efforts hope they will:

- Lead to faculty synergies in both research and education
- Take advantage of cross-cultural fertilization and enhanced creativity
- Appeal to a larger number of prospective students, and
- Appeal to corporations, in turn attracting executive education dollars

Internal Corporate Education Centers

Rather than wait for universities to turn out better-prepared students, many corporations have brought education inhouse. Such corporate centers have been dubbed "corporate universities" or CUs. Lawrence Tapp (then Dean of the Richard Ivey School of Business in Canada) put it thus: "A real corporate university is where business strategy, organizational culture and human resource development meet, blend, and synthesize—and performance takes off." [17] Some corporations have concluded they can provide their employees with the right tools faster than universities; others have concluded that it's better to co-brand the internal effort with a recognized university, rather than doing all the work inhouse. This generally means creating a unique curriculum offered inhouse, in collaboration with university professors who often participate as instructors at these CUs, along with company executives and professional trainers. CUs have also become very good prospective employers for PhD graduates who've elected to leave academia.

E-learning, Technology, and the Demise of the Traditional Classroom

The traditional view that education is the exclusive playground of physical "brick and mortar" schools has been seriously challenged over the past decade; dozens of firms have entered the education market and now provide a plethora of online "distance learning" solutions. Traditional universities, recognizing the business imperative of keeping up with these new entrants, have implemented new technology and innovative distribution mechanisms in response.

Many observers of the technology boom have hoped advances in Internet technology will help to achieve greater parity in education quality. Advances in Internet and web broadcasting solutions are very promising in helping some schools narrow the gap—when students and professors in smaller schools suddenly have access to the collective knowledge of the rest of the world, it cannot help but open their eyes, provide them with the tools and motivate them to raise the scholastic bar locally.

The largest private university in North America today is the University of Phoenix, which offers almost 200 locations, as well as Internet delivery in most countries globally.[18] According to Wikipedia, the university has an enrollment of over 345,000.

Money Matters

Traditional Sources of Funding

In the United States, as in many countries, government provides large subsidies for public education; public institutions of higher learning depend on donations to supplement dwindling government funding. Private universities are even more dependent on donations.

Traditional sources of funding for academic institutions include:

- Tuition payments by students
- Government subsidies for education

- Government grants for research
- Nongovernmental (not-for-profit) organization research grants
- Corporate grants
- Endowed chairs
- Private donations, and
- Corporate donations

Government deficits, particularly due to the global financial crisis, have meant cutbacks of public funding for education; periods of economic contraction correlate with reductions in the number and size of donations and grants by individuals and corporations. The financial belt-tightening is relative, as some schools and departments are better off than others.

Traditional Inequities

The most obvious, and frequently debated, inequity is the growing disparity between the wealthiest private academic institutions and, effectively, all public institutions. Anthony Bianco, in a December 2007 *BusinessWeek* article, documented "The Dangerous Wealth of the Ivy League." Wealthy schools can expend billions of dollars on state-of-the-art facilities and recruiting the brightest academic stars. Public schools, who simply cannot compete with the wealthier schools, watch their star professors being steadily snapped up at salaries they cannot conceive of matching. This inequity may well become more pronounced if governments cut back funding even further for public universities due to the adverse effects of the economic crisis on budgets.

A second type of inequity—the relative wealth of Faculties—is often found *within* universities; some Faculties and departments such as business, law, and medicine are able to attract significant funding, while others must rely on steadily dwindling government support and philanthropic organizations. Recessionary periods tend to limit both sources of support considerably.

Some academicians are able to generate additional income from book sales and consulting fees. Predictably, their ability to do so depends on the prestige of their institution, and the extent to which their field of specialization lends itself to commercial applications. One young faculty member in an Ivy League psychology department was so frustrated with his inadequate pay he toyed with the idea of selling advertising space on his class overheads! He also considered selling billboard space on the front of the podium he used for lecturing.

Needless to say, as scholarly institutions focus more on the greenback, there is growing concern that they are focusing too little on scholarship. A case in point is discussed by Jason Allen in a *Wall Street Journal* article:[19] "Despite shaky economic times, and criticism from academic quarters, major colleges around the country are on a construction binge, spending huge sums to build and expand stadiums and gyms." Supporters claim the incoming funds from paying fans and TV contracts help the entire university, while critics charge that the money stays in the athletics departments, and doesn't reach other programs. The full truth is likely somewhere between the two positions. What matters, however, is that every minute spent on these debates is one less minute spent on scholarship.

Affirmative Action and Diversity

This book cannot do justice to such a controversial and emotionally charged debate as affirmative action. The purpose here is simply to discuss affirmative action as *one* major agenda item of institutions of higher learning. Beyond being an important issue to society, legal rulings on this controversial issue may well affect one's ability to get into a doctoral program, receive funding, and obtain employment.

Affirmative action was instituted following acknowledgement that minority applicants were at a disadvantage due to prejudice, and/or because they didn't have access to the life experiences or preparatory exercises needed to compete for admission to the best institutions. The idea behind the various affirmative action programs instituted across the nation was that they were meant to level the playing field—to give those who had the deck stacked against them a fighting chance. It was thought that once a generation of minorities had this enhanced access, they would realize economic success and would, in turn, be in a position to open up opportunities for their descendants, who would no longer require the affirmative action.

From its inception, however, affirmative action was criticized as being nothing short of "reverse discrimination." Members of the majority became increasingly frustrated that "their" admissions spots for universities, government contracts, and jobs were being given to "less-qualified" minority applicants. They voiced concerns they were being discriminated against because employers and schools had to fill quotas in certain minority groups, and that race was being used in these decisions—a notion they claimed was at odds with legal principles.

Good or bad, the fact remains that affirmative action has been under assault around the country. Several legal challenges against affirmative action have succeeded, forcing institutions of higher learning to amend their policies. The debate is intense and likely to continue for years to come.

Affirmative action isn't a uniquely American effort. According to *The Economist*,[20] affirmative action efforts directed at overcoming exclusion due to the caste system led to a decade of rioting in India during the 1980s. Britain's class system has also been blamed for stacking the deck against members of the less-privileged social classes. The article reports that in an effort to remedy the situation, the British government gave a "postcode premium" of five percent on grants to schools for each student from a poor area. The article goes on to argue that discriminating against intelligent people, who are worthy of university positions, based on their having a certain wealthy-looking postal code isn't the solution to society's ills. Rather, the focus should be on having a national screening system in place which does a better job of identifying intelligent students, across all classes, and giving them equal opportunity to enter the country's university system.

Although it gets very little press, there is yet another type of preferential treatment in admissions. The name sometimes given to this type of admission is "development admits." *The Wall Street Journal*[21] describes this practice of giving preferential admissions treatment to students from wealthy families: the universities' expectations are that the students' parents will subsequently donate money to the institutions. Backers of this policy explain that the funds raised from these parents are used to improve facilities and extend scholarships to other students. Critics point out that the majority of students accepted under this allowance come from white families, another example of how disadvantaged certain minority applicants are, and yet another reason why affirmative action is so sorely needed.

Tenure Erosion and Part-Time Professorships

One of the most sought-after aspects of the academic life has always been attaining tenure. While highly advantageous for the person receiving tenure, "someone" has to foot the bill for these cushy arrangements, and this "someone" is the academic institution, or, for public schools, the taxpayers. Budget cuts have forced many institutions to reexamine the value they receive from their tenured faculty; tenure is extremely expensive. The natural outcome has been a gradual move to granting fewer tenured positions, coupled with ongoing efforts to reduce the benefits of tenure to individual faculty members.

Many institutions now offer a watered-down version of tenure, and many also seek to use more visiting, part-time, and adjunct professors. The teaching and research communities have been fighting back tooth and nail, on all fronts. There are efforts to restore tenure rights and privileges to their old glory, and other efforts to grant tenure to people ineligible under current rules.

The bottom line is, as always, dictated by the availability of funding. Those schools with resources are able to maintain support standards, while those feeling the financial pinch find themselves increasingly disadvantaged.

Grade Inflation

Grade inflation, the steady upward trend in university grades, has been observed at the college level over the past few years, to the point where large percentages of graduating classes in some leading universities are all "A" students. The upward drift has been attributed to at least three factors:

1. University administrations seeking to please parents and students who pay tens of thousands of dollars to attend college
2. Professors attempting to give their students a better chance at good jobs
3. Professors making exams and coursework especially easy in hopes this will avoid conflicts with students and ensure favorable teaching reviews

A 2002 article in Canada's *Globe and Mail* newspaper[22] highlights grade inflation in a leading institution:

> More than 50% of Harvard students were finishing courses with grades of A or A-. Last year an extraordinary 91 percent of Harvard students were also given some type of honors on their diploma, about three times the rate of other Ivy League universities.

In the article's concluding paragraph, a student is quoted as saying:

> My parents are paying more than $100,000 for me to be here at Harvard. For that kind of investment I expect to have marks that make an employer look at my transcript and say, "Wow."

The paper notes that an influential Harvard academic committee recently recommended that grading be addressed with the aim of making "B" the *average* grade, rather than "C," as in most grading schemes.

Intellectual Property Rights

One of the most contentious issues between academics and their employers (universities) is intellectual property rights, and, in particular, who owns them. Most institutions lay claim to those rights, under the argument that the institution empowers the researcher and pays her salary, providing research support in the form of assistants, laboratories, and a community of like-minded scholars to spur research and innovation. In some cases researchers are allocated a share of royalties.

The researchers themselves, not surprisingly, also lay claim to the innovations, declaring that their unique contributions of skill and knowledge create the innovations, and failure to recognize their property rights effectively makes them slaves working for the enrichment of the institution. They argue that taking ownership away from them removes incentives and leads to reduced innovation.

This promises to be a lively debate for years to come.

Chapter 12: Application to a PhD Program

It takes a special kind of commitment to survive a doctoral program. Intense intellectual work, limited income, and lack of time for family and friends may stretch over at least half a decade; overcoming each of the ever-more-difficult academic challenges is no guarantee of ultimate success. Determination that you have the passion and commitment to take on these challenges is the first step. The next step is the actual application to doctoral programs. The typical process is described below.

Formal Application Requirements

The following are required in order to be considered for acceptance into a typical graduate program in the United States:

- The General Requirements Examination or GRE. Some departments also require special sections of the GRE, specific to the intended course of study. A Graduate Management Admissions Test or GMAT or other exam may also be acceptable.
- Transcripts showing an outstanding academic record in previous bachelor's and/or master's work.

- Several essays, including an explanation of why the applicant is interested in the particular program and why she believes she will succeed.
- Two or more reference letters.
- Interviews. These aren't always necessary.
- Samples of relevant work: for arts programs, musical compositions or copies of paintings; performing arts programs may require live demonstrations, recitals or auditions.
- Fluency in a second language, for humanities programs in particular.
- An application fee.

Application packages, sent to and received by the various universities' program administrators, are checked for completeness, then forwarded to the admissions committee.

Other than situations requiring interviews or auditions, it's all done but the waiting. Weeks and months can go by, making the waiting more and more difficult; applicants stew and wait while the admissions committee reviews applications.

The Admissions Committee

The admissions committee is comprised of a handful of professors who are appointed or volunteer to evaluate applications and select an incoming class of graduate students. They typically work with one or several of the program's administrators.

Most schools use a number of filters to evaluate qualifications among the applicant pool. First they look at grade point averages, standardized test scores, and whether applicants have the appropriate background. This first sweep ensures the survivors are at least somewhat intelligent and possess basic prerequisites in analytical capabilities and relevant subject matter. A practical example of background relevance is that it's virtually impossible to be admitted to a graduate program in chemistry if the applicant has never taken a chemistry course in his life.

The initial sweep may eliminate all but fifty of the hundreds of applicants; those weeded out receive rejection letters. Many students can't take the wait or have other deadlines, and call in for an update on the status of their application. The fortunate ones will be told they're still in the running; those less fortunate will be told they did not make the initial cut. Some administrators are defensive, fearing a verbal, or worse, attack by applicants who refuse to accept a rejection. In this light, their preference for an arms' length rejection-by-mail is a bit more understandable.

There is no point in arguing with or pestering admission committee members: such immature behavior can only hurt the applicant's case, not help it; no amount of arguing will lead a committee to reverse a decision to reject an applicant. An example which perhaps explains this rule involved a prospective student who was rejected by an Ivy League economics department. His employers at a government agency pleaded his case and succeeded in gaining his admission. Less than a year later the student dropped out of the program, harming the reputation of his government supporters and the university administrators who made the exception in his case.

It's important to ask why an application was rejected, take disappointing feedback constructively, and apply the learning to improve one's chances with other schools.

The admissions committee examines the remaining applicant pool more closely; they weigh the credibility and enthusiasm of the reference letters, and try to learn more about each person's abilities and motivation, based on his course of study and essays. Several dozen more applicants are weeded out at this stage and notified by mail. With just a few dozen applicants left, some schools invite applicants in for interviews; other schools proceed without interviews. Interviews can be very useful in evaluating applicants, but are also time-consuming and expensive: personal meetings may reveal certain characteristics—age, gender, appearance, religion—it's illegal to consider in the application process. Some schools prefer the anonymity of the no-interview process, as it protects them against discrimination lawsuits. You can't be accused of religious discrimination if you've never been in a position to identify the person's faith.

Eventually, the selection committee puts together a short list of admitted applicants, and a waiting list of applicants. Schools determine the number of incoming positions available, usually based on available budgets and instructors. Some schools make a few more offers than they have positions, as they expect some offers to be turned down. If too many of the original offers are turned down, the open spots will be offered to those on the waiting list.

Many schools make fewer offers than their original allotment if they believe the candidate pool is particularly weak, their logic being that admitting people who seem inadequate is not the best use of limited resources.

The school is obligated to honor all offers accepted, even if a larger class than originally anticipated is admitted. This isn't necessarily bad from the school's perspective, as it now has many students with high potential. Incoming students, however, may find a much more competitive environment where they must compete for limited resources. Departments may purposely set examinations at a more difficult level to "reduce enrollment" after the first year.

Intangible Requirements

In addition to the basic filters of good grades and satisfactory standardized test scores, admissions committee members look for less tangible characteristics that don't show up on a grade sheet—traits that separate those destined to be called "Professor" from those who won't survive the rigors of the greatest intellectual challenge our system of education has to offer. Most admissions committees look for the following, in no particular order:

- The ability to remain unwaveringly and passionately focused on a singular objective
- The maturity to accept criticism constructively, and

- The creativity and intellectual ability to add new knowledge to their field

One of the most important assessments made by the committee has to do with commitment and likelihood of successful completion of the program. Passion for the chosen subject and demonstrated willingness to work hard are minimum requirements: the department and faculty will expend significant resources (intellectual and emotional energy, time, and money) on each admitted student. Students are expected to be committed enough to succeed in the program and earn a respectable tenure-track position following graduation. A person with a PhD is forever associated with his doctoral program *alma mater*. One of the first questions exchanged by people with PhDs is where each attended her PhD program. Academically successful, well-respected graduates are a source of prestige the PhD-granting institution can always claim.

Given the significant commitment made to each student, it's often disappointing to the department when one fails to complete the program or defects to a nonacademic position. PhD program administrators want to be convinced that everyone in an incoming class is committed to completing the program and realizing success within the academic community. If anyone suspects the student is simply seeking a free master's degree (often granted after a year or two in the doctoral program), he will be rejected.

Application Strategy

Decision making begins the moment one begins to complete applications. Which schools to apply to? Does one aim high, applying to only the best schools? What if all respond with rejections? That would mean waiting another year before applying again to other schools. Is it sensible, then, to apply to many schools with very different reputations? The process can be very expensive and time-consuming. Each program's requirements are different, requiring each application package to be specifically tailored so that economies of scale are difficult to realize. Each application may also require a fee of fifty to one hundred dollars. So, does one give up on the better, typically more expensive schools, and apply to the more local state-supported schools? The process has barely begun, yet it is already maddening!

A fairly common recommendation is to apply to two or three "reach" schools from which acceptance is unlikely but conceivable; the various schools that are likely to grant admission and you would like to attend, and two "safety" schools which are almost certain to grant admission. The latter become relevant in the event none of the preferred applications are successful. Don't apply to schools you have no interest in attending, even as fallback options.

For many who planned to apply to graduate school from the time they were undergraduates, the stress begins even earlier. Every exam they take during their undergraduate studies feels like it has enormous implications. Many students believe one poor exam grade may lead to a poor course grade, which in turn will "destroy" their grade average and doom them to being shut out of their chosen field of study, or their favorite graduate school. This creates a tremendous amount of pressure—unnecessary pressure.

An applicant must manage to get one message across clearly—she has a passion for the field. Here is an example of what *not* to say:

> I've always liked math and I was very good at it in school. My high school teacher said I should be a math professor. I really want to be a math professor.

Tangible proof of interest comes across much more convincingly from the following:

> When I was in third year of my BSc in math I was a research assistant for Professor Jones. As part of this collaboration, I wrote programs which searched for perfect numbers and created graphical displays of Bessel functions using Matlab. In my fourth year, I

explored Gaussian properties and spent two months in the summer working with Professor Smith. I found it necessary to learn to program in SAS for the project.

These are, obviously, fabricated examples. The first example reflects a person who *fancies* herself an academic, the second reflects a person who is truly interested in and committed to being an academic. The first example shows no curiosity, no passion, and no real effort; the second example demonstrates all of these qualities; the applicant has made a conscious effort to vary her experiences, driven by genuine, burning curiosity.

An ideal way to explore a subject is by working with a researcher. This is sufficiently important that a student should consider doing so even without compensation (although the experience is more genuine if the student's effort is seen as valuable enough to justify payment). Attaining a PhD requires years of commitment and hard work. Sacrificing a few months to find out whether the longer commitment is worthwhile may be the best investment a student ever makes. If she discovers she isn't cut out for the academic life, she just saved herself a lot of time, energy, and anxiety—and she has an interesting experience to list on her résumé. If she finds her inner fire is kindled even more, she will gain confidence and conviction that will stand her in good stead on her chosen path.

Another important element of the application should be an effort to seek out professors in schools the student is considering, and discuss mutual interests. Professors probably won't have much time, but the good ones will respond and encourage students if they sense talent and sincerity. The tricky part is to *find* the good ones; some prospective students interact with faculty and are turned off by lack of responsiveness and impatience.

A young student with a bachelor's degree is unlikely to "wow" a professor with his knowledge of a subject, so it's best not to try too hard: intensity and commitment to make one's studies the number one priority are necessary to gain the professor's confidence and support.

An ideal way to gain experiences with faculty interactions is by applying for teaching or research assistantships at their current college (whether pursuing a bachelor's or master's degree). Discussing personal interests with professors already familiar with a student's work, and who appear sympathetic and inclined to give honest feedback, is an excellent start. Typically, these professors will be the ones providing letters of recommendation, and a good word from them can make the difference in admissions to other schools, or lead to acceptance in the *alma mater*'s graduate school, which can be very efficient.

Graduate students in target institutions are usually less intimidating to speak with than faculty, and can provide the "inside scoop" on the program. Speaking with students at different stages of the program, and gauging the quality of their experiences at the school is also useful. Some will be receptive to talking, so consider what you really need and want to know, make a list of questions, and be mindful of your source's time constraints. Some PhD students may be arrogant and play the "I got in while you're one of the huddled masses" power game. Ignore them.

Scholars "talk shop" by publishing their findings, so reading what they have to say can be most enlightening. Investigating the field's most important peer reviewed publications is a critical step in entrance applications: academic journals represent the academic community marketplace, where ideas are shared and debated. Applicants must read journal articles as early as possible to discern whether they are appealing and at least somewhat stimulating: if the articles are too dry or abstract, beware! Graduate students are required to read hundreds of such articles, and probably thousands over the course of an academic career. If a student really can't stand the subject and writings at such an early stage, research in general or research in the particular field may not be a satisfying career. Perhaps a more practitioner-oriented or professional degree is a better choice.

Admission Granted

After months of waiting, the phone will ring and the good news will be conveyed by one of the school's faculty members or administrators—"admission granted." In some cases the good news is delivered by mail or email.

There are, of course, several possible reactions: delight or relief at being accepted into this particular program, or indifference about this institution—not thrilled about it, but willing to attend. This may have been an institution applied to as an afterthought, but never really considered an option. Be polite on the phone, no matter who calls, no matter what your initial opinion of the school may be. It is never good to create a poor impression, because the academic community is quite a small place. The best thing to do when that call comes is thank the caller genuinely and ask any relevant questions.

Another possibility is an offer of admission to a less-than-thrilling program or university; if there is sufficient time to defer a decision, it is best to do so and await responses from other schools. Most universities allow at least a few weeks for applicants to make their final decision. If no better offers are forthcoming, the best option is to visit the school a second time; a particular school may not have seemed very impressive initially, but a second visit may dispel that notion. You may find the people in the department wonderfully helpful and cooperative, the place quaintly appealing with a small-college-town atmosphere, and the professors highly approachable and genuinely interested in their students.

The best outcome, of course, is being thrilled at the acceptance. A visit to the school as soon as possible is useful; a school's reputation may precede it, but it would be reckless to accept a position without getting a firsthand look at the facilities, and speaking to professors and graduate students. A visit can confirm a choice or raise questions: it's best to clear up outstanding concerns early in the process.

There may be any number of negative aspects to the school; it's important to identify them early on, and it may be legitimate to decline the offer. Is it acceptable for a student with deep passion for a subject to turn down a school because it is not the most credentialed, or is in a region where one can't consider living? This is a very personal decision. Passion is a necessary component for success, but realism is also relevant. If an applicant is concerned that job prospects will be severely hampered by attending a particular school, or has concerns about his family's safety or happiness in a particular location, declining the offer may be the correct choice.

Another dimension to the decision is the level of funding or support included in the acceptance. A typical dilemma is gaining acceptance to two schools: a highly rated school offering no or limited funding, and a less well-known school offering a full scholarship. Which graduation scenario is better: a prestigious degree with $100,000 of personal debt, or a less prestigious, debt free degree? Prevailing wisdom is to seek the most prestigious degree, but in practical terms, the difference in prestige may not be very large, employment prospects not very different, and the looming debt load a significant barrier to personal financial freedom.

Many schools, particularly the better ones, have a few days set aside for entertaining admitted students who have not yet committed to the school in an effort to sell them on the idea. Good schools make a concerted effort to enroll the best graduate students; they may even pay for the students' travel expenses for the event. The best students are an investment in the school's future, as their eventual success reflects well on the school and continues to propagate its reputation. Formal visitation events typically include an orientation session, during which a dean may speak in inspiring fashion about the school, a tour of the campus, several one-on-one sessions with certain professors, possibly a wine and cheese event, sessions with enrolled graduate students, and perhaps a dinner or luncheon with a selection of faculty members and/or students.

Whether your visit is formal or informal, make time to meet the (frequently neglected) department support staff: receptionists, secretaries, deans' assistants, office managers, and IT support personnel. These people are critically important to your ability to navigate the program. Gauge their level of cooperation, and begin to foster positive relationships with them by being polite and considerate; too many incoming students make the mistake of taking on airs of superiority with respect to support personnel. Avoid bad manners: first, it just isn't right to be a snob to anyone! Second, remember that these people control many of the resources you will need over five or more years; if they perceive you as undeserving of their best efforts, you may find your time in the program frustrating at best. If neither reason seems compelling, do the rest of us a favor and redirect your career away from academics—you're exactly the kind of person we'd like to see less of because you can create a very unhappy environment.

Speak with as many students as you can and ask them about their experiences. Find out what they are happy with in the program, and what has disappointed them; discuss academic and nonacademic issues—housing, campus atmosphere, department politics, local entertainment, where to find the best sandwiches.

Relationships with faculty members are critical to your success; to be useful to you, they need to be accessible and to care about their students. Your progression through the program will depend on the quality of your rapport. Your funding, in many programs, will come from your faculty mentor, advisor, dissertation committee chair or principal investigator. Do everything you can to gauge the level of respect faculty give to students. A good measure is how they interact with other faculty members, students and support staff. Just open your ears in a mingling session and get a feel for the conversations around you—is there a fun, friendly, collegial atmosphere? Is the setting tense, with professors appearing to come in for a few minutes just because the department chairman ordered them to attend? Do they appear genuinely interested in the new crop of potential students? Keep in mind that some of your most intimate and reliable sources of information may be the younger faculty members, who still remember being in your shoes.

Chapter 13: Questions Applicants Should Ask Prior to Accepting Admission Offer

The decision to attend a particular school shouldn't be taken lightly. The time spent evaluating a school by phone queries, through web searches, or during site visits is a scarce resource and should be used responsibly. One's focus should be on collecting sufficient information to answer the following questions:

- Are the faculty members credible?
    a. Are they approachable?
    b. Are they good teachers?
    c. Do they care about their students?
    d. Will they be good mentors and partners during the dissertation phase?
- Is there a critical mass of faculty?
    a. Are there enough professors within the department who can become mentors and collaborators?
    b. If the student's interests evolve, will there be other faculty to work with?
    c. If one's principal advisor leaves the school, will someone else be available to take her place?

- Are the other students helpful?
    a. Is there an atmosphere of cooperation, or
    b. Unhealthy competition?
- Is the department sufficiently financially endowed to offer good facilities?
- Will the financial support be sufficient for survival?
- What is the placement record of PhD graduates?
    a. Do they obtain good academic positions?
    b. Are those positions in good schools, or lesser ones?
- How many years have students been at the school?
    a. Many students in their sixth year and beyond can be a danger signal.
    b. Is there a common denominator among the longer-term students?
- Will one's family be happy living in the particular location?
- Is the school's medical insurance acceptable?

To respond to these questions, concentrate on the following during the research phase and site visit:

- School's reputation. It's a fact of life that some universities are better than others, better able to equip their graduates for jobs and life's other challenges. The best schools are wealthier, have better facilities, and average a larger concentration of established professors (who can be mentors and or future collaborators in research). Several well-known schools that attract the most prestige, the best professors, and the best students are England's Cambridge and Oxford, Japan's Tokyo and Kyoto Universities, Russia's Moscow State University, and the United States' Ivy League schools, along with Stanford, MIT, Northwestern, and a handful of others (who will undoubtedly greatly resent being left off this list). The school's reputation must be taken into account because it *does* make a difference. Yes, one can reach the pinnacle in the field by being good, regardless of which school one attends, but the simple fact is that graduates of better-known schools tend to get more postdoctoral and employment opportunities.

- Computing and IT facilities. At first glance the extent of these facilities may not be obvious. Some departments have a special computer lab for graduate students; others don't, forcing graduate students to share time with a large population of undergraduate students. The quality of the technology may also vary across schools and departments. The wealthier schools and departments are more likely to have newer computers, more printers and scanners, better access to useful software packages, and more likely to have IT support specialists on hand. Thus, a private, wealthy, Ivy League university is more likely to have better resources than a small public school in a less-populous region. But there can be exceptions: during my graduate student days (over a decade ago), I discovered that a medium-sized university in Ontario, Canada, had far-superior technology in its graduate student lab than the PhD student computer cluster of an Ivy League institution.

- Financial aid package. It's very important to fully understand the terms of support. An applicant must be able to survive financially—be able to focus on studying without constantly worrying about making ends meet, and having to interrupt the education process working to put food on the table. Financial aid may include grants, loans, teaching and research assistantships. It's important to get a complete picture of the available sources of funding before committing to a decision.

- Health insurance. This is especially critical in the United States, whose health care system differs quite significantly from those of many other countries. The applicant must ensure that he and his family are comprehensively covered; this is nonnegotiable. Few interruptions are more frightening and devastating than severe health problems. If a school's health insurance offerings are not sufficient, it may be possible to supplement them with other sources.

- Program structure. One of the most trying aspects of a PhD program is the lack of structure compared to undergraduate programs; lack of structure leads to a sense of uncertainty, disorienting many students. Some schools have a special reputation for providing little guidance to their students—intimidating to students who prefer their hands held a bit more. Gauge the philosophy a given department has with regard to structure, and compare that to personal preferences. Each department may have its own philosophy, but individual professors may deviate significantly from departmental norms. A good person to speak with is the department chair, but take her comments with a grain of salt as she may be telling you what she thinks you want to hear in the hope you accept the offer. As with many other topics, your best sources of unfiltered information are graduate students within the program.

- Humanity of faculty members. Conscientious applicants read articles written by faculty members to gauge professors' professional interests and capabilities, but journal articles say little about them as people. Are they approachable? Do they have a sense of humor? Do they respect their colleagues and support staff? Do they communicate openly and enthusiastically? Is there a happy, constructive atmosphere?

- Facilities relevant to program of study. A student considering a physical chemistry program should take a look at the graduate student labs, and the undergraduate laboratories where he may be required to teach. Laboratories are important in other subjects such as biology and neurosciences. Physics students may have a need to check out particle accelerators, clean rooms, and even nuclear reactors if relevant to their course of study. Arts students should see the studios, music students need to test the acoustics of practice rooms, and everyone needs to know the proximity of their places to coffee and sandwiches.

- On-campus housing. How costly are the options? How easy is it to get to the department's office? Do graduate students have office space? How comfortable is that space?

- Schools and employment opportunities for spouse. Day care facilities and employment opportunities are critical if your spouse supports the family.

- Neighborhood safety. It's a sad fact that some of America's best universities are situated in unsafe neighborhoods; several institutions are making efforts to help fix their neighborhoods and security image, but it is still necessary for the student to identify the safer locations.

- Grant availability. In many fields (chemistry, biology, physics) much of the funding for facilities and student salaries comes from grants, and students must participate in the grant writing process. Applicants should assess whether this particular activity is approached constructively; one immunology graduate jokingly introduced herself as the "administrative assistant." When I asked why, she explained that her typical day was spent putting together grant applications, photocopying them in quintuplicate, and walking them to the nearest FedEx center—a far cry from the more glamorous vision she had of the world of science.

- Teamwork requirement. PhD students come from very different personal backgrounds: some have families and many associated responsibilities, while others may be very young and have no external obligations. This diversity can affect everyone positively or negatively: a married student with family may not want to stay very late at school. For programs of study that are very individual, this isn't an issue because the student's choice will affect his individual performance only, but in some fields where work is done collectively in a laboratory or studio setting, this means more work for those who remain behind, and forces them to stay even later. Some students make a conscious decision not to have a family so they can concentrate on work, and they understandably feel it's unfair that they have to carry the load for others. If you expect to enroll in a program where teamwork is required, do your best to gauge what the rest of the team will be like.

- Athletic facilities. Graduate programs are generally very stressful and a good way to vent this stress is adopting/continuing healthy habits, including sufficient exercise. Athletic facilities vary in importance, depending on the applicant's hobbies and inclinations; but, all else held equal, better facilities in better locations do count for something, particularly if students have spouses or family who use the gyms or playing fields.

- Houses of worship. Depending on the applicant's needs for a community of faith, the availability of, and proximity to, houses of worship may be important.

Chapter 14: Conclusion

The decision to pursue a PhD is a momentous one. Any PhD program is very difficult, and requires great sacrifice, passion and commitment. While undeniably difficult, the process is enlightening, exciting, and rewarding. The effort is likely to last about five years, and affect the student and her entire family. It's a significant undertaking that challenges people constructively, but also makes them question their own commitment and self-worth, and, in some cases, drives them to the verge of insanity.

The decision to become a member of this distinguished community brings with it social responsibility. Along with one's fellow scholars, the new PhD is charged with some of humanity's most prized possessions: the integrity of the scientific method, championing freedom of thought, opinion, exploration, expression, speech and the education of future generations of scholars and thought leaders.

As you embark on the highest challenge offered by the higher education system, keep in mind that obtaining the PhD is only the beginning.

Tables

Table 1: Top 20 Doctorate-Granting American Institutions, by Broad Field of Study, 2007

Institution	Number of Doctorate Recipients
University of California, Berkeley	896
University of Michigan	783
University of Minnesota	778
University of Texas-Austin	778
University of Wisconsin-Madison	773
University of California, Los Angeles	719
University of Illinois-Urbana-Champaign	693
Harvard University	690
Pennsylvania State University	685
Stanford University	684
Ohio State University	664
University of Florida	647
University of Maryland	645
Purdue University	609
MA Institute of Technology (MIT)	601
University of Washington	592
University of Southern California	584
Texas A&M University	580
Cornell University	485
University of Pennsylvania	484
All Fields	48,079

Source: NSF/NIH/USED/NEH/USDA/NASA, *2007 Survey of Earned Doctorates*, National Opinion Research Center (NORC).

Table 2: Number of Doctorate Recipients by Major Field of Study in the United States for Selected Years, 1992–2007

Field of Study	1992	1997	2002	2007
Life Sciences	7,172	8,421	8,478	10,630
Physical Sciences	6,444	6,581	5,604	8,037
Social Sciences	6,481	7,285	6,826	7,191
Engineering	5,438	6,115	5,081	7,745
Education	6,677	6,577	6,503	6,429
Humanities	4,176	5,190	5,221	5,109
Other Fields	2,498	2,370	2,311	2,938
All Fields	38,886	42,539	40,024	48,079

Source: NSF/NIH/USED/NEH/USDA/NASA, *2007 Survey of Earned Doctorates*, National Opinion Research Center (NORC).

Table 3: Number of Doctorate Recipients in the United States, by Sex, within Broad Field of Study for Selected Years, 1992–2007

Field of Study and Sex	1992	1997	2002	2007
All Fields [a]	38,670	42,187	39,943	48,025
Male	24,234	24,944	21,807	26,166
Female	14,436	17,243	18,136	21,859
Life Sciences [b]	7,141	8,367	8,466	10,617
Male	4,322	4,614	4,443	5,163
Female	2,819	3,753	4,023	5,454
Physical Sciences [c]	6,399	6,528	5,595	8,028
Male	5,133	5,082	4,103	5,775
Female	1,266	1,446	1,492	2,253
Social Sciences [d]	6,450	7,215	6,813	7,186
Male	3,353	3,404	3,041	2,971
Female	3,097	3,811	3,772	4,215
Engineering	5,368	6,067	5,069	7,734
Male	4,861	5,317	4,175	6,133
Female	507	750	894	1,601
Education	6,664	6,517	6,490	6,428
Male	2,688	2,394	2,196	2,097
Female	3,976	4,123	4,294	4,331
Humanities	4,165	5,154	5,211	5,103
Male	2,236	2,693	2,599	2,585
Female	1,929	2,461	2,612	2,518
Other Fields	2,483	2,339	2,299	2,929
Male	1,641	1,440	1,250	1,442
Female	842	899	1,049	1,487

[a] Group totals exclude individuals for whom sex was not reported; 216 in 1992, 352 in 1997, 81 in 2002, and 54 in 2007; [b] Includes agricultural sciences/natural resources, biological/biomedical sciences and health sciences; [c] Includes mathematics and computer & information sciences; [d] Includes psychology.

Source: NSF/NIH/USED/NEH/USDA/NASA, *2007 Survey of Earned Doctorates*, National Opinion Research Center (NORC).

Table 4: Citizenship Status of Doctorate Recipients in the United States, by Broad Field of Study for Selected Years, 1992-2007

Citizenship Status	1992	1997	2002	2007
All Doctorates	38,886	42,539	40,024	48,079
U.S. Citizen	26,023	28,154	26,050	27,568
Permanent Resident of U.S.	1,974	2,932	1,662	1,832
Temporary Visa Holder in U.S.	9,980	9,192	9,743	15,115
Unknown	909	2,261	2,569	3,564

Source: NSF/NIH/USED/NEH/USDA/NASA, *2007 Survey of Earned Doctorates,* National Opinion Research Center (NORC).

Table 5: Top 25 Countries/Economies of Origin of Non-U.S. Citizens Earning Doctorates at U.S. Colleges and Universities, 2007

Rank	Country/ Economy	Number of Recipients
1	China, including Hong Kong	5,002
2	India	2,228
3	Korea	1,529
4	China, Rep. of (Taiwan)	755
5	Canada	629
6	Turkey	559
7	Japan	330
8	Thailand	275
9	Russia	269
10	Germany	237
11	Mexico	229
12	Romania	209
13	Brazil	180
14	Great Britain, UK	174
15	France	173
16	Iran	163
17	Italy	147
18	Argentina	141
19	Jordan	132
20	Egypt	127
20	Israel	127
22	Greece	125
23	Colombia	123
24	Spain	121
25	Kenya	95

Source: NSF/NIH/USED/NEH/USDA/NASA, *2007 Survey of Earned Doctorates,* National Opinion Research Center (NORC).

Table 6: Median Number of Years from Beginning of Graduate Work to Doctorate Award, by Broad Field of Study, for Selected Years, 1992–2007

Field of Study	1992	1997	2002	2007
All Fields	8.7	8.7	8.6	7.8
Life Sciences [a]	7.9	7.7	7.4	7.1
Physical Sciences [b]	6.9	6.9	6.7	6.8
Social Sciences [c]	8.7	8.2	8.2	7.9
Engineering	7.1	7.2	7.2	6.9
Education	15.6	15.7	14.2	12.0
Humanities	10.2	9.7	9.7	9.3
Other Fields	10.9	10.7	10.7	9.3

[a] Includes agricultural sciences/natural resources, biological/biomedical sciences and health sciences.

[b] Includes mathematics and computer & information sciences.

[c] Includes psychology.

Source: NSF/NIH/USED/NEH/USDA/NASA, *2007 Survey of Earned Doctorates*, National Opinion Research Center (NORC).

Table 7: Number of Faculty, Average Salary (in USD), Average Total Compensation (in USD), and Percent of Faculty Tenured, by Academic Rank, 2007–2008

Category or Rank	Number of Faculty	Average Salary	Average Comp.	Percent Tenured
Professor	116,749	102,867	129,976	94
Associate	97,847	72,961	94,191	82.7
Assistant	100,340	61,103	78,918	7.3
Instructor	23,969	44,533	58,327	1.9
Lecturer	22,608	49,846	65,381	1.5
No Rank	5,963	56,245	72,625	1.5
Totals	367,476	75,677	96,956	54.1

Note: The table is based on 1,386 (salary) and 1,374 (compensation) reporting institutions.

Source: The Annual Report on the Economic Status of the Profession, 2007–08. American Association of University Professors (AAUP), www.aaup.org

Table 8: Number of Degree-Granting Institutions Conferring Degrees, by Control and Level of Degree: 2005-06

Control Type	Associate's	Bachelor's	Master's	Doctor's
Public Institutions	1,299	602	510	248
Private Institutions	1,369	1,612	1,148	374
Total	2,668	2,214	1,658	622

Source: National Center for Education Statistics, U.S. Department of Education, 2005–06 Integrated Postsecondary Education Data System (IPEDS), Fall 2006.

Table 9: Endowment Funds of the 20 Colleges and Universities with the Largest Endowments, by Rank Order, 2005 and 2006.

NOTE: Between 2006 and mid-2009, endowment values increased sharply, then lost on average 25-30% of their peak values due to the global slowdown, declining roughly to their 2006 levels.

Institution	Rank Order[1]	Market Value of Endowment as of June (in millions)	
		2005	2006
Total for 120 schools with largest endowments		$234,940	$268,899
Harvard University	1	25,473	28,915
Yale University	2	15,224	18,030
Stanford University	3	12,205	14,084
University of Texas System	4	11,610	13,234
Princeton University	5	11,206	13,044
MA Inst. of Tech (MIT)	6	6,712	8,368
Columbia University	7	5,190	5,937
University of California	8	5,221	5,733
University of Michigan [2]	9	4,931	5,652
Texas A&M University [2]	10	4,963	5,642
University of Pennsylvania	11	4,369	5,313
Northwestern University	12	4,215	5,140
Emory University	13	4,376	4,870
University of Chicago	14	4,137	4,867
Washington University	15	4,268	4,684
Duke University	16	3,826	4,497
University of Notre Dame	17	3,650	4,436
Cornell University	18	3,777	4,321
Rice University	19	3,611	3,986
University of Virginia	20	3,219	3,618

[1] Institutions ranked by size of endowment in 2006. [2] Includes foundations.

Source: National Center for Education Statistics, U.S. Department of Education, *Digest of Education Statistics*, 2007.

Notes

[1] "Doctor of Philosophy" *The Columbia Encyclopedia*, 6th ed. (New York: Columbia University Press, 2001–07). www.bartleby.com/65/. September 9, 2008.

[2] Jon A. Krosnick, "What Americans Think about Climate Change," presented at American Psychological Association session entitled *Symposium: Psychology of Global Climate Change*, August 2008, Boston.

[3] Anders Henriksson, comp. *Non Campus Mentis: World History According to College Students* (New York: Workman Publishing Company, 2001).

[4] Debbie Schlussel, "Professor Miami Vice," February 2002. http://www.politicalusa.com/columnists/schlussel/archives.htm#16

[5] Sharon Dolovich, "Making Docile Lawyers: An Essay on the Pacification of Law Students," *Harvard Law Review* 111, no. 7 (1998), 2027-2044.

[6] These descriptions are primarily based on information found in *Wikipedia* online.

[7] "Professor" *Online Etymology Dictionary*, http://www.etymonline.com/index.php?term=professor, September 9, 2008.

[8] Jonathan D. Glater, "Pay Packages for Presidents Are Rising at Public Colleges," *New York Times,* November 20, 2006.

[9] Julie N. Lynem, "Industry Outlook, Education: A Hard Row," *San Francisco Chronicle,* May 19, 2002.

[10] "Is There Any Truth to Today's Résumés?" *USA Today,* February 4, 2003.

[11] Stacey Humes-Schultz, "Business Schools Suffer Post-Enron Soul-Searching," *Financial Times,* July 12, 2002.

[12] "Reality Check: Alleged Fraud Gets Physicists Thinking About Misconduct," *Scientific American,* November 2002, 20-22.

[13] "Yale Site Hacked," *The Australian,* July 31, 2002.

[14] "Fellowships Help Plug Brain Drain," *The Australian,* July 31, 2002.

[15] Thomas H. Benton, "The 7 Deadly Sins of Students," *Chronicle of Higher Education,* April 14, 2006. http://chronicle.com/jobs/news/2006/04/2006041401c/careers.html.

[16] Thomas H. Benton, "The 7 Deadly Sins of Professors," *Chronicle of Higher Education,* May 12, 2006. http://chronicle.com/jobs/news/2006/05/2006051201c/careers.html.

[17] Lawrence Tapp, "Business Strategy of Cooperation and Learning," *The Financial Times,* March 25, 2002.

[18] http://www.phoenix.edu/about_us/about_us.aspx

[19] Jason Allen, "Colleges Bulk Up Spending on Stadiums," *Wall Street Journal,* July 31, 2002.

[20] "Affirmative Action, Negative Reaction," *The Economist,* March 8, 2003.

[21] "Extra Credit: At Many Colleges, the Rich Kids Get Affirmative Action," *Wall Street Journal*, February 20, 2003.

[22] "Why Harvard Hates Straight A's," *Globe and Mail*, Toronto, April 22, 2002.

References

Books & Magazines

Bianco, Anthony. 12-10-2007. The dangerous wealth of the ivy league. *Businessweek*.

Debelius, Maggie, and Basalla, Susan Elizabeth. 2001. *So what are you going to do with that? A guide for MA's and PhD's seeking careers outside the academy*. New York: Farrar, Straus and Giroux.

Diamond, Jared. 1997. *Guns, germs, and steel: The fates of human societies*. New York: W. W. Norton & Co.

Glazer-Raymo, Judith. 2008. *Unfinished agendas: New and continuing gender challenges in higher education*. Baltimore, Johns Hopkins University Press.

Goleman, Daniel. 2005. *Emotional intelligence: Why it can matter more than IQ*. New York: Bantam.

Goleman, Daniel. 2000. *Working with emotional intelligence*. New York: Bantam.

Gray, John. 1992. *Men are from Mars, Women are from Venus.* New York: Harper Collins.

Henriksson, Anders, ed. 2001. *Non campus mentis: World history according to college students.* New York: Workman Publishing Company.

Newhouse, Margret. 1993. *Outside the ivory tower: A guide for academics considering alternative careers.* Office of Career Services: Harvard University.

Pink, Daniel H. 2006. *A whole new mind: Why right-brainers will rule the future.* New York: Riverhead Books.

Sacks, Oliver. 2001. *Uncle Tungsten: Memories of a chemical boyhood.* New York: Alfred A. Knopf.

Sullivan, William H., Rosin, Matthew S., Shulman, Lee S., and Fenstermacher, Gary D. 2008. *A new agenda for higher education: Shaping a life of the mind for practice.* San Francisco: Jossey-Bass.

Zinn, Howard. 2003. *A people's history of the United States: 1492-Present.* New York: HarperCollins.

Websites

Please note: Site descriptions are, for the most part, taken verbatim from the respective websites.

AcademicKeys.com, offers universities a venue to efficiently recruit for higher-level faculty and administrative positions in the engineering fields. http://engineering.academickeys.com/

American Association of University Professors (AAUP), advances academic freedom and shared governance, defines professional values and standards for higher education.
http://www.aaup.org/aaup

Arts and Letters Daily: A service of the Chronicle of Higher Education.
http://www. aldaily.com

Association for Support of Graduate Students. http://www.asgs.org/

Association to Advance Collegiate Schools of Business International (AACSB) is devoted to the promotion and improvement of higher education in business administration and management.
www.aacsb.edu

Chronicle of Higher Education, source of news, information, and jobs for college and university faculty members and administrators.
http://www.chronicle.com

The Delta Project's mission is to help improve college affordability by controlling costs and improving productivity.
http://www.deltacostproject.org/resources/news.asp

Digest of Education Statistics. http://nces.ed.gov/programs/digest/d07/tables/ dt07_001.asp

Edge Foundation, Inc. Promotes inquiry into and discussion of intellectual, philosophical, artistic, and literary issues, as well as to work for the intellectual and social achievement of society.
http://www.edge.org

Improbable Research. Strives to make people *laugh*, and then make them *think*. It administers the Ig Nobel prizes, to celebrate the unusual, honor the imaginative, and spur people's interest in science, medicine, and technology. http://www.improb.com/

Inside Higher Ed is the online source for news, opinion and jobs for all of higher education. http://insidehighered.com/

Life Essentials offers life and dissertation coaching services. http://www.lifeessentialscoaching.com/

National Academies, comprised of the entities listed below, provide science, technology and health policy advice under a congressional charter.
http://www7.nationalacademies.org/resdoc/index.html
National Research Council.
http://sites.nationalacademies.org/nrc/index.htm
National Academy of Engineering. http://www.nae.edu/
National Academy of Sciences.
http://www.nasonline.org/site/PageServer
Institute of Medicine. http://www.iom.edu/

National Association of Graduate and Professional Students. http://www.nagps.org/

National Center for Education Statistics (NCES) is the primary federal entity for collecting and analyzing data related to education. It is located within the U.S. Department of Education and the Institute of Education Sciences. http://nces.ed.gov/

National Center for Higher Education Management Systems' mission is to improve strategic decision making in higher education for states and institutions in the United States and abroad. http://www.nchems.org/

National Center for Public Policy and Higher Education promotes public policies that enhance Americans' opportunities to pursue and achieve high-quality education and training beyond high school. http://www.highereducation.org/

National Education Association. www.nea.org

National Opinion Research Center.
http://www.norc.org/issues/docdata.htm

The PhD Project's mission is to increase the diversity of corporate America by increasing the diversity of business school faculty. http://www.phdproject.org/

PhinisheD, A discussion and support group for people trying to finish their dissertations. http://www.phinished.org/

Review of Higher Education provides a forum for discussion of varied issues affecting higher education. The journal advances the study of college- and university-related topics through peer reviewed articles, essays, reviews and research findings. http://www.press.jhu.edu/journals/review_of_higher_education/

Science, Math, and Engineering Career Resources. http://www.phds.org/

Scholars at Risk Network (SAR) promotes academic freedom and defends the human rights of scholars and their communities worldwide. http://scholarsatrisk.nyu.edu/Beta/

Slashdot. News for Nerds. Stuff that Matters. http://science.slashdot.org

U.S. Census Bureau, Current Population Survey. http://www.census.gov/cps/

Index

73, 82, 83, 85, 96, 99, 103,
104, 123, 124, 130, 131, 134,
137, 138, 139, 171, 177, 183,
184, 187, 189, 191, 193

defense, 33, 35, 46, 51, 52, 53,
63, 68, 100, 115, 123, 154

deficit, 169

degree, 3, 6, 40, 48, 50, 59, 71,
83, 100, 120, 179, 181, 182,
184

delay, 10, 54, 59, 131

democratic, 135

demographer, 129

department, 11, 12, 13, 14, 15,
16, 18, 21, 30, 35, 36, 41, 44,
45, 58, 78, 79, 89, 90, 93, 94,
95, 96, 97, 120, 121, 123, 124,
137, 138, 139, 140, 141, 147,
148, 149, 152, 153, 158, 166,
169, 170, 175, 177, 179, 183,
184, 185, 187, 188, 189, 190,
191

depression, 64, 73

design, 108, 156

development, 27, 33, 37, 77,
115, 167, 171

discipline, 26, 63, 64, 102, 108,
114

discovery, 4, 14, 23, 36, 45, 65,
66, 74, 116, 129, 130, 133,
149, 155

discrimination, 171, 178

discussion, 14, 16, 74, 86, 117,
130, 145

dishonest, 151, 157

dismissal, 71, 116

dissertation, 6, 22, 23, 25, 26,
33, 34, 39, 41, 43, 45, 46, 47,
48, 49, 50, 51, 52, 53, 54, 55,
57, 63, 65, 67, 68, 69, 71, 77,

78, 79, 81, 85, 89, 90, 93, 95,
100, 185, 187

dissertation committee, 26, 33,
34, 39, 41, 43, 49, 51, 52, 67,
68, 85, 89, 93, 185

dissertation proposal, 33, 45,
46, 48, 63

distance learning, 168

distraction, 5, 149

diversity, 170

Doctor, 3, 79

Doctor of Philosophy, 3

doctoral studies, 3

doctorate, 119

doctrine, 155

dogma, 115, 150

donate, 172

donation, 168, 169

Douglas Harper, 121

draft, 30, 36, 47

ears, 109, 185

earth, 114, 134, 150, 160

eccentric, 154, 155

economic, 108, 115, 129, 169,
170, 171

economics, 110, 111, 130, 143,
148, 160, 177

economist, 103, 129

economy, 102

editor, 10, 130, 131, 133, 160

editorial board, 30, 130

education, 1, 5, 18, 57, 59, 60,
98, 100, 112, 113, 114, 115,
117, 118, 119, 120, 127, 129,
136, 138, 140, 147, 156, 161,
162, 165, 166, 167, 168, 169,
178, 189, 193

educator, 118, 138

effect, 29, 108, 109, 166

ego, 133, 149, 156

E-learning, 166, 168
electrical, 120
elementary, 164
elite, 112
email, 9, 10, 17, 90, 151, 183
embarrassment, 20, 21, 67, 70, 73, 89
emeritus professor, 45, 122
emotional competence, 65
empathy, 65
empirical, 13, 30, 45, 74, 96
employer, 84, 86, 87, 89, 91, 93, 100, 167, 171, 173, 174, 177
employment, 6, 31, 35, 36, 39, 44, 57, 58, 81, 84, 85, 86, 89, 90, 91, 92, 93, 100, 101, 102, 103, 135, 136, 141, 142, 153, 157, 170, 184, 189, 191
energy, 12, 35, 50, 64, 81, 94, 179, 181
engineering, 58, 82, 101, 105, 120, 130, 147, 165
English, 83, 110, 164
enlightenment, 115, 155
enrollment, 20, 63, 168, 178
Enron, 157
entertainment, 185
environment, 20, 22, 33, 40, 78, 84, 105, 109, 110, 117, 128, 143, 165, 178, 185
essay, 176, 177
ethics, 5, 17, 36, 156, 157, 158
etiquette, 132
Europe, 3, 52, 121, 155
evidence, 50, 102, 108, 113, 149
examination, 11, 12, 19, 20, 22, 23, 24, 43, 46, 58, 67, 69, 73, 74, 100, 128, 173, 175, 178, 180
excommunication, 115

executive, 82, 167
exercise physiology, 130
exotic, 61
experience, 21, 25, 27, 30, 31, 47, 58, 66, 71, 74, 75, 78, 85, 89, 94, 101, 104, 117, 144, 148, 152, 165, 181
exploration, 46, 48, 114, 115, 193
expression, 5, 84, 107, 114, 115, 193
extracurricular, 75
extremism, 150, 156
eyes, 13, 54, 109, 168
facility, 74, 97, 98, 99, 109, 121, 122, 147, 148, 158, 159, 169, 172, 183, 188, 189, 191, 192
faculty, 4, 10, 12, 14, 15, 16, 18, 26, 27, 30, 31, 35, 37, 41, 44, 45, 46, 50, 68, 69, 74, 82, 84, 89, 94, 96, 97, 99, 109, 115, 120, 122, 136, 137, 139, 140, 141, 148, 151, 154, 156, 158, 160, 165, 167, 170, 172, 179, 181, 182, 184, 185, 187, 190
Faculty, 15, 58, 120, 121, 138, 140, 147, 148, 153, 158, 169
faculty club, 99
Faculty of Engineering, 120
fail, 3, 4, 5, 20, 22, 29, 38, 40, 49, 51, 52, 59, 68, 70, 71, 72, 74, 95, 104, 109, 133, 143, 161, 174
failure, 4, 20, 22, 38, 40, 49, 51, 70, 71, 72, 74, 95, 104, 109, 133, 174
fallacy, 115
family, 5, 18, 22, 40, 41, 42, 59, 72, 73, 75, 83, 136, 139, 175, 184, 188, 189, 191, 192, 193

fanatical, 115

fauna, 128, 150

faux pas, 20

fear, 70, 136, 156, 157

fee, 13, 57, 143, 144, 170, 176, 180

feedback, 25, 26, 27, 28, 29, 30, 37, 46, 65, 68, 70, 89, 92, 96, 131, 139, 177, 182

Fidel Piety, 116

field, 4, 10, 13, 14, 25, 29, 30, 33, 39, 43, 44, 46, 48, 50, 52, 63, 65, 77, 81, 83, 87, 88, 91, 92, 94, 97, 100, 103, 111, 130, 131, 132, 133, 134, 135, 142, 150, 154, 158, 160, 170, 171, 179, 180, 182, 189

fieldwork, 37

finance, 82, 83, 122, 123, 160

financial, 5, 6, 19, 26, 58, 59, 67, 72, 79, 82, 83, 96, 108, 123, 130, 143, 145, 147, 169, 172, 184, 188

financial aid, 58, 123, 189

Financial Times, 157

financing, 61

fire, 116, 136, 166, 181

first author, 36, 132, 135

flexibility, 65

flora, 128, 150

focus, 5, 10, 14, 25, 36, 65, 66, 69, 86, 87, 90, 107, 118, 139, 150, 152, 170, 171, 187, 189

food, 12, 99, 113, 122, 189

fraternity, 156

fraternization, 43, 153

fraud, 158

freedom, 5, 44, 101, 107, 114, 115, 128, 136, 155, 156, 184, 193

French, 84, 130

fringe, 130

frustration, 23, 64, 65, 69

full professor, 45, 101, 122, 124

fundamentalist, 150, 156

funding, 15, 30, 37, 38, 44, 59, 60, 61, 79, 97, 98, 101, 120, 122, 128, 137, 141, 147, 152, 168, 169, 170, 172, 184, 185, 189, 191

fund-raising, 79, 123, 147

fusion, 110

future, 4, 15, 26, 27, 34, 38, 44, 60, 73, 83, 97, 100, 107, 112, 114, 116, 135, 136, 141, 144, 156, 164, 166, 184, 188, 193

gain, 1, 21, 28, 29, 89, 108, 123, 156, 181

galaxy, 148

Galileo Galilei, 150

gender, 6, 177

General Requirements Examination, 175

generals, 164

genius, 105, 127

gesture, 16, 27

global, 155, 164, 165, 167, 169

goal, 4, 35, 88, 90, 104

god, 10, 41, 114, 116, 117, 142, 155

governance, 122

Governing Board, 122

government, 15, 30, 58, 60, 81, 82, 88, 100, 101, 102, 108, 111, 113, 115, 119, 120, 122, 128, 143, 145, 147, 168, 169, 171, 177

grade inflation, 161, 173

grade-point average, 19

grading, 15, 31, 173

location, 28, 89, 97, 158, 184, 188

logic, 45, 59, 68, 72, 86, 115, 153, 178

logical, 114, 129

logistics, 99

loneliness, 73

mainstream, 66

maintenance, 13, 122, 123, 124

majority, 88, 132, 152, 171, 172

managers, 120, 121, 122, 123, 166

manuscript, 10, 15, 29, 53, 54, 132

margin, 53

Mark Twain, 129

Massachusetts Institute of Technology, 147

master, 25, 26, 41, 42, 63, 65, 71, 98, 100, 119, 124, 175, 179, 182

material, 11, 14, 21, 23, 24, 25, 27, 28, 30, 49, 63, 64, 68, 69, 98, 109, 132, 148, 165

maternity, 21

mathematics, 113, 148

maturity, 5, 23, 64, 68, 178

MBA, 6, 165

MD, 6

measure, 64, 109, 111, 112, 113, 114, 132, 149, 185

mechanical, 89, 120

media, 108, 157

medical, 57, 63, 147, 159, 160, 188

medicine, 4, 6, 58, 120, 124, 147, 165, 169

medieval, 3, 52

mediocre, 82, 86, 163

meeting, 14, 15, 16, 142

mental capacity, 5

mental health, 73

mentor, 6, 33, 34, 35, 79, 118, 185

methodology, 45, 109, 146

Middle East, 156

milestones, 24

military, 58

minority, 58, 60, 150, 152, 170, 171, 172

minutes, 9, 14, 15, 16, 88, 111, 185

misery, 72

mistake, 35, 70, 113, 116, 162, 184

model, 102, 108, 162

molecules, 150

momentum, 65, 115, 158

money, 4, 30, 31, 45, 58, 59, 79, 114, 138, 143, 145, 160, 161, 164, 168, 170, 172, 179

moon, 114

moral fiber, 5

morale, 21, 64

mortarboard, 155

Moses, 116

motivation, 64, 98, 115, 177

motive, 103, 108, 143

music, 120, 190

myth, 109

Napoleon, 155

nation, 115, 117, 129, 157, 171

National Opinion Research Center, 3

nationalism, 150

natural, 4, 22, 23, 34, 43, 69, 71, 88, 103, 109, 110, 120, 148, 172

natural sciences, 110, 120

Nobel, 36, 48, 130, 142, 143,

policy, 111, 172
political, 46, 108, 123, 130, 132, 140, 141, 142, 150, 151
postdoctoral fellow, 77, 78, 79
poster, 29, 131, 144, 146
posture, 27
praise, 163
prejudice, 38, 170
preliminary, 19, 22, 23, 25, 46, 91, 115
preparation, 5, 11, 20, 21, 22, 35, 89
prerequisite, 5, 20, 66, 71, 78, 176
presentation, 16, 27, 28, 29, 31, 52, 67, 69, 74, 77, 84, 88, 89, 92, 95, 144, 145, 146
presentation skills, 66
president, 47, 120, 121, 122, 136
pressure, 11, 18, 26, 48, 69, 73, 90, 151, 156, 157, 180
prestige, 30, 79, 83, 91, 94, 109, 124, 129, 132, 135, 137, 138, 141, 143, 150, 159, 170, 179, 184, 188
prestigious, 10, 29, 57, 58, 83, 86, 117, 124, 130, 140, 142, 143, 145, 146, 160, 184
Princeton, 117, 158
principal investigator, 6, 22, 33, 35, 41, 53, 79, 185
private, 30, 37, 57, 83, 85, 101, 104, 120, 124, 147, 159, 168, 169, 189
procedure, 21, 52, 110, 132
productivity, 4, 130
professional, 6, 27, 34, 35, 65, 74, 79, 87, 90, 94, 139, 144, 165, 167, 182, 190

professor, 9, 116, 117, 121, 149, 178, 180
proof, 65
prosperity, 107
provost, 121
psychology, 108, 110, 170
public, 15, 28, 57, 69, 82, 108, 120, 122, 124, 143, 146, 156, 159, 168, 169, 172, 189
public opinion, 108
publication, 10, 17, 18, 25, 29, 35, 38, 77, 78, 79, 85, 87, 96, 123, 128, 130, 131, 132, 133, 134, 137, 140, 142, 148, 151, 182
publish or perish, 66, 127, 129
purists, 143
qualifying, 23, 26, 60, 65
quality, 1, 29, 54, 84, 86, 87, 94, 98, 99, 112, 128, 130, 133, 138, 140, 147, 148, 162, 164, 165, 166, 168, 182, 185, 189
quantitative analysts, 112
quota, 171
race, 139, 171
reading list, 11, 12, 25, 69
reading skills, 66
real estate, 82
receptionist, 184
recession, 111, 170
recital, 176
recommendation, 16, 85, 86, 180, 182
recruiter, 81, 84, 85, 86, 90, 93
recruiting, 18, 84, 88, 90, 92, 95, 96, 99, 141, 169
rector, 120, 121
reference letter, 36, 84, 85, 86, 87, 92, 93, 176, 177
reform, 115

registration, 13, 144
rejection, 92, 93, 139, 177, 179
relationship, 26, 34, 35, 36, 37,
  38, 39, 40, 41, 43, 77, 113,
  144, 152, 153, 184
reliability, 109, 110
religion, 116, 117, 150, 155, 177
religious, 115, 155, 156, 178
repression, 115, 150
reprisals, 116
reputation, 38, 39, 58, 67, 135,
  177, 183, 184, 188, 190
research assistant, 9, 12, 26, 58,
  97, 180, 181, 189
research fund, 12, 31, 44
researcher, 6, 31, 94, 110, 113,
  118, 130, 131, 132, 133, 134,
  140, 160, 174, 181
resource, 4, 18, 30, 37, 41, 43,
  46, 64, 74, 97, 104, 147, 148,
  152, 165, 166, 167, 172, 178,
  179, 184, 187, 189
responsibility, 51, 107, 116, 118,
  130, 133, 153, 158, 162, 163,
  193
resubmit, 10
résumé, 84, 85, 86, 90, 181
retention, 19, 66, 82
reviewer, 29, 131, 133, 134
revision, 10, 12, 15, 17, 51, 52,
  131, 133
rigorous, 63, 83, 103, 108, 109,
  116, 130, 132, 160
risk, 38, 67, 68, 143
romance, 152, 153
roundtable, 145
royalty, 55
sabbatical, 136
sacrifice, 100, 134, 193
safety net, 74

salary, 78, 79, 82, 83, 91, 97,
  124, 141, 174
schedule, 24, 38, 92, 139
schizophrenia, 154
scholar, 15, 29, 73, 115, 116,
  119, 120, 128, 130, 134, 150,
  151, 155, 159, 160, 174, 193
scholarship, 4, 44, 57, 58, 60,
  65, 119, 123, 155, 160, 170,
  172, 184
science, 4, 46, 83, 110, 111, 121,
  129, 130, 133, 138, 158, 191
Scientific American, 158
scientific discovery, 74, 107
scientific method, 109, 193
scientific process, 108
scientist, 44, 78, 82, 107, 110,
  129, 132, 151, 155, 159, 164
scrutiny, 16, 133
secretaries, 124, 184
secretary, 124, 184
secular, 155
security, 30, 102, 107, 122, 135,
  136, 153, 191
selector, 92
self-esteem, 101, 163
seminal, 150, 154
seminar, 16, 36, 89, 96
sense of humor, 190
September 11, 159
service, 12, 58, 82, 115, 137,
  140, 160
setback, 64, 73, 74
sex, 42, 152, 153
Sharon Dolovich, 117
Shepherd College, 116
signature, 53, 55
significance, 52, 69, 109, 112
significant, 4, 19, 22, 23, 33, 44,
  49, 58, 63, 69, 71, 73, 74, 81,

83, 101, 102, 104, 112, 118,
130, 132, 133, 135, 137, 138,
148, 150, 151, 169, 179, 184,
193

silence, 52, 116

sin, 28, 50

skepticism, 65

skill, 20, 27, 29, 30, 31, 34, 44,
63, 64, 65, 66, 77, 82, 84, 87,
88, 91, 95, 101, 102, 104, 109,
123, 124, 142, 143, 155, 164,
165, 174

social, 20, 22, 36, 61, 83, 95,
104, 108, 110, 111, 113, 115,
120, 128, 142, 150, 171, 193

social sciences, 22, 83, 110, 111

society, 1, 4, 5, 6, 33, 42, 46, 82,
107, 108, 115, 116, 119, 127,
129, 137, 150, 162, 164, 166,
170, 171

sociologist, 129

sociology, 113

soft, 111

software, 97, 189

Southeast Asia, 156

space, 14, 97, 147, 148, 149,
170, 191

speaker, 13, 70, 88, 96, 144, 145

speaking engagements, 131,
143, 144

special interest groups, 108

specialization, 48, 143, 170

speculative, 131

speech, 114, 115, 136, 155, 193

sports, 111, 160

spouse, 142, 152, 153, 191, 192

SSHRC, 60

stadium, 170

staff, 14, 17, 52, 95, 98, 102,
122, 124

standard, 12, 16, 36, 43, 44, 89,
129, 130, 131, 156, 158, 160,
163, 172

standard of living, 129

standardized test, 71

Stanford, 147, 188

state, 5, 14, 15, 53, 60, 78, 82,
120, 155, 159, 169, 180

statistical, 87, 112

stereotype, 154

stigma, 73

stock market, 110

stockbroker, 82

stress, 25, 26, 29, 64, 68, 69, 73,
74, 147, 152, 180, 192

structure, 6, 25, 29, 41, 44, 48,
49, 69, 84, 102, 164, 190

student, 42, 43, 68, 73, 74, 98,
121, 156

Student Affairs, 121

student housing, 123

student services, 121

studio, 22, 97, 191

study, 6, 19, 21, 24, 29, 34, 43,
48, 52, 63, 67, 74, 81, 82, 83,
87, 97, 108, 110, 122, 134,
146, 153, 164, 175, 177, 180,
190, 191

subfield, 134, 152

subject, 5, 9, 11, 16, 35, 38, 43,
45, 64, 65, 66, 67, 69, 82, 83,
90, 101, 108, 109, 130, 140,
145, 147, 152, 159, 176, 179,
181, 182, 183

submission, 10, 51, 53, 54, 55,
130, 131, 132, 133

submission requirements, 55,
131

subsidy, 168

success, 5, 22, 23, 26, 28, 40, 42,

urgent, 15, 104
vaccine, 111
valedictorian, 157
validity, 109, 110, 150
Van Gogh, 110
varsity, 16
vice, 163
Vietnam War, 115
virtual, 129, 162
virus, 25
visa, 159
vision, 44, 191
visiting professor, 52
vulnerable, 115
waiting list, 93, 178
waiver, 26, 58, 99

Wall Street, 83, 112, 170, 171
warning, 86, 115
waste management, 122
wealthy, 83, 91, 122, 147, 159,
    171, 172, 189
Wernher Von Braun, 127
Wikipedia, 119, 168
Wilson Mizner, 156
world, 1, 5, 14, 39, 47, 48, 49,
    59, 69, 70, 72, 77, 78, 92, 93,
    100, 101, 115, 122, 127, 129,
    131, 133, 134, 135, 149, 150,
    151, 154, 155, 158, 159, 160,
    164, 168, 191
Yahoo, 116
Zorro, 117

Contacting Yuval Bar-Or

Yuval Bar-Or is the founder and president of the Light Brigade Corporation, which owns and administers several websites:

www.respectrisk.com – an educational resource on risk, risk-taking, and risk mitigation.

www.leadershiprisk.com – a site dedicated to leadership, leadership risk, and leadership development.

www.creditsolutionsdemystified.com – a site dedicated to credit risk management solutions; catering to an international clientele primarily in the financial services industry.

Yuval Bar-Or may be reached through the **Contact Us** screen of any of these websites.

Also Available from Author Yuval Bar-Or
and TLB Publishing

Leveraging People for a Corporate Turnaround

Leadership and Management Guidance
for Organizational Change

Yuval Bar-Or

January 2009

www.tlbcorp.com

Breinigsville, PA USA
19 October 2009
226118BV00004B/19/P